ANALYSIN QUANTITATIVE DATA

for BUSINESS *and* MANAGEMENT STUDENTS

SAGE was founded in 1965 by Sara Miller McCune to support the dissemination of usable knowledge by publishing innovative and high-quality research and teaching content. Today, we publish more than 750 journals, including those of more than 300 learned societies, more than 800 new books per year, and a growing range of library products including archives, data, case studies, reports, conference highlights, and video. SAGE remains majority-owned by our founder, and after Sara's lifetime will become owned by a charitable trust that secures our continued independence.

Los Angeles | London | Washington DC | New Delhi | Singapore

ANALYSING QUANTITATIVE DATA

for BUSINESS and MANAGEMENT STUDENTS

CHARLES A. SCHERBAUM & KRISTEN M. SHOCKLEY

Los Angeles | London | New Delhi
Singapore | Washington DC

Los Angeles | London | New Delhi
Singapore | Washington DC

SAGE Publications Ltd
1 Oliver's Yard
55 City Road
London EC1Y 1SP

SAGE Publications Inc.
2455 Teller Road
Thousand Oaks, California 91320

SAGE Publications India Pvt Ltd
B 1/I 1 Mohan Cooperative Industrial Area
Mathura Road
New Delhi 110 044

SAGE Publications Asia-Pacific Pte Ltd
3 Church Street
#10-04 Samsung Hub
Singapore 049483

Editor: Kirsty Smy
Assistant editor: Nina Smith
Production editor: Sarah Cooke
Copyeditor: Sharon Cawood
Proofreader: Lynda Watson
Indexer: Judith Lavender
Marketing manager: Catherine Slinn
Cover designer: Francis Kenney
Typeset by: C&M Digitals (P) Ltd, Chennai, India

Library of Congress Control Number: 2014943646

British Library Cataloguing in Publication data

A catalogue record for this book is available from
the British Library

ISBN 9781446273524
ISBN 9781446273531 (pbk)

At SAGE we take sustainability seriously. Most of our products are printed in the UK using FSC papers and boards.
When we print overseas we ensure sustainable papers are used as measured by the Egmont grading system.
We undertake an annual audit to monitor our sustainability.

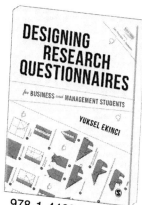

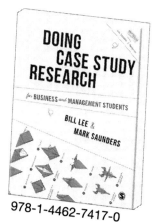

CONTENTS

EDITORS' INTRODUCTION TO THE *MASTERING BUSINESS RESEARCH METHODS* SERIES

Welcome to the *Mastering Business Research Methods* series. In recent years, there has been a great increase in the numbers of students reading masters level degrees across the business and management disciplines. A great number of these students have to prepare a dissertation towards the end of their degree programme in a time-frame of three to four months. For many students, this takes place after their taught modules have finished and is expected to be an independent piece of work. Whilst each student is supported in their dissertation or research project by an academic supervisor, the student will need to find out more detailed information about the method that he or she intends to use. Before starting their dissertations or research projects these students have usually been provided with little more than an overview across a wide range of methods as preparation for this often daunting task. If you are one such student, you are not alone. As university professors with a deep interest in research methods, we have provided this series of books to help students like you. Each book provides detailed information about a particular method to support you in your dissertation. We understand both what is involved in masters level dissertations, and what help students need with regard to methods in order to excel when writing a dissertation. This series is the only one that is designed with the specific objective of helping masters level students to undertake and prepare their dissertations.

Each book in our series is designed to provide sufficient knowledge about either a method of data collection or a method of data analysis, and each book is intended to be read by the student when undertaking particular stages of the research process, such as data collection or analysis. Each book is written in a clear way by highly respected authors who have considerable experience of teaching and writing about research methods. To help students find their way around each book, we have utilized a standard format, with each book having been organized into six chapters:

- **Chapter 1** introduces the method, considers how the method emerged for what purposes, and provides an outline of the remainder of the book.
- **Chapter 2** addresses the underlying philosophical assumptions that inform the uses of particular methods.
- **Chapter 3** discusses the components of the relevant method.
- **Chapter 4** considers the way in which the different components may be organized to use the method.
- **Chapter 5** provides examples of published studies that have used the method.
- **Chapter 6** concludes by reflecting on the strengths and weaknesses of that method.

We hope that reading your chosen books helps you in your dissertation.

Bill Lee, Mark NK Saunders and VK Narayanan

ABOUT THE SERIES EDITORS

Bill Lee, PhD is Professor of Accounting and Head of the Accounting and Financial Management Division at the University of Sheffield, UK. He has a long-standing interest in research methods and practice, in addition to his research into accounting and accountability issues. Bill's research has been published widely, including in: *Accounting Forum*; *British Accounting Review*; *Critical Perspectives on Accounting*; *Management Accounting Research*; *Omega*; and *Work, Employment & Society*. His publications in the area of research methods and practice include the co-edited collections *The Real Life Guide to Accounting Research* and *Challenges and Controversies in Management Research*.

Mark NK Saunders BA MSc PGCE PhD FCIPD is Professor of Business Research Methods in the Business School at the University of Surrey, UK. His research interests are research methods, in particular methods for understanding intra organisational relationships; human resource aspects of the management of change, in particular trust within and between organisations; and small and medium-sized enterprises. Mark's research has been published in journals including *Journal of Small Business Management*, *Field Methods*, *Human Relations*, *Management Learning* and *Social Science and Medicine*. He has co-authored and co-edited a range of books including *Research Methods for Business Students* (currently in its sixth edition) and the *Handbook of Research Methods on Trust*.

VK Narayanan is the Associate Dean for Research, Director of the Center for Research Excellence, and the Deloitte Touché Stubbs Professor of Strategy and Entrepreneurship in Drexel University, Philadelphia, PA. His articles have appeared in leading professional journals such as *Academy of Management Journal*, *Academy of Management Review*, *Accounting Organizations and Society*, *Journal of Applied Psychology*, *Journal of Management*, *Journal of Management Studies*, *Management*

Information Systems Quarterly, *R&D Management* and *Strategic Management Journal*. Narayanan holds a bachelor's degree in mechanical engineering from the Indian Institute of Technology, Madras, a post graduate degree in business administration from the Indian Institute of Management, Ahmedabad, and a Ph.D. in business from the Graduate School of Business at the University of Pittsburgh, Pennsylvania.

ABOUT THE AUTHORS

Dr Charles A. Scherbaum is an Associate Professor of Psychology at Baruch College and the Graduate Center of the City University of New York. His research focuses on personnel selection, cognitive ability testing, attitudes toward stigmatized employees and applied psychometrics. He received his PhD in industrial and organizational psychology from Ohio University. His research focuses on personnel selection, cognitive ability testing, attitudes toward stigmatized employees, test validation, analytics and applied psychometrics. Publications of his research have appeared in journals such as *Personnel Psychology*, *Organizational Research Methods*, *Educational and Psychological Measurement*, *Journal of Business and Psychology* and *Leadership Quarterly*, and in numerous chapters in edited books. His research has been supported by the National Science Foundation and the Graduate Management Admission Council. Charles was one of the winners of the 2011 M. Scott Myers Award for Applied Research from the Society for Industrial and Organizational Psychology (APA Division 14). Charles is on the editorial boards of the *Journal of Applied Psychology* and the *Journal of Business and Psychology*. He is the past president of the *Metropolitan New York Association for Applied Psychology*.

Dr Kristen M. Shockley is an Assistant Professor in the Psychology Department at Baruch College and the Graduate Center of the City University of New York. She received her PhD in industrial and organizational psychology from the University of South Florida. Her main area of research focuses on understanding the intersection of employees' work and family lives. Specifically, she has conducted research aimed at understanding organizational initiatives to help employees manage competing life demands (i.e. flexible work arrangements); research that explores the relationship between work–family conflict and health outcomes, including eating behaviours and physiological indicators of health; research that addresses the measurement and theoretical foundations of work–family interactions; and research targeted at understanding how dual-earner couples balance work and family roles. Her research has been published in several journals, such as the *Journal of Vocational Behavior*, *Journal of Management*, *Human Performance*, *Journal of Occupational Health Psychology*, *Journal of Mixed Methods Research* and *Personnel Psychology*, and in numerous chapters in edited books. Her scholarly work has been awarded through the Society for Industrial/Organizational Psychology's 2010 Mary L. Tenopyr and the 2012 S. Rains Wallace awards. She enjoys teaching Introduction to Statistics at both undergraduate and masters levels.

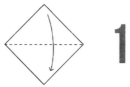

1

INTRODUCTION

Quantitative data and analysis have become an integral part of research and business (*Economist*, 2010; Salsburg, 2002; Siegel, 2013). Many scholars and observers have claimed that we are now living in the age of 'big data' and quantitative analysis (e.g. McAfee and Brynjolfsson, 2012) and that the nature of research and business are transforming as a result (e.g. Ayers, 2008; Davenport and Harris, 2007; Siegel, 2013). In fact, it has become impossible to navigate today's academic literature or business media without encountering at least some mention of 'big data' and quantitative analysis. News stories about how quantitative data analysis is being used to fundamentally change some aspect of research, business or life seem to appear daily. Books about the successful use of quantitative analysis, such as Michael Lewis's (2004) *Moneyball*, have become 'required' reading in many areas of business.

The excitement currently being generated by quantitative data analysis is easy to understand, given the impact that quantitative data and analysis have made on a number of fields ranging from professional sports, to medicine, to internet search, to management, to operations and to marketing. The benefit of this renewed interest is that new methods, software, books, websites, conferences and information are proliferating at an astounding rate. For those interested in quantitative data and analysis, these are exciting times.

While exciting, the times are changing for all researchers and practitioners. It appears that we have reached a tipping point where knowledge of quantitative data analysis is no longer optional for most areas of research and many areas of business. We question whether one can be successful in research or industry without some competence in understanding, using and interpreting quantitative data analysis. Countless reports and surveys point to the conclusion that there is a great demand for individuals with knowledge and skill in quantitative data analysis, but these individuals are in short supply. Some have gone as far as claiming that jobs in quantitative analysis will become one of the most desirable and prestigious careers in the 21st century (Davenport and Patil, 2012).

Even for those that are knowledgeable and skilled in quantitative data analysis, the development and proliferation of tools and methods have made the decision about what one should do an exceedingly challenging one. We find that the most common question asked by experienced researchers and practitioners is, 'How does one determine which analyses are the most appropriate for the data and research method?' Ultimately, the choice of the appropriate quantitative analysis will be based on the purpose of the research (e.g. exploratory or confirmatory), the research questions being asked (and the associated hypotheses to be tested), the research design (e.g. experimental or non-experimental) and the nature of the data (e.g. scale of numerical measurement, shape of the distribution; Scherbaum, 2005). Yet, making these decisions can still be exceedingly difficult because of the unwieldy array of information and options that must be considered in choosing quantitative analyses.

The challenge, especially for students, also stems from the difficulty associated with developing a framework or mental model for understanding quantitative analyses. Quantitative analyses are not simply a set of techniques to be applied to data. Rather, they are a way of systematically thinking about research questions, research methodology and the observed patterns in the data. One could even consider quantitative analysis a language that allows researchers to communicate using an agreed upon vocabulary. It is this mental model of quantitative analysis that serves as an invaluable aid in making choices about appropriate analyses, research methodology and research questions.

The aim of this book is to assist students, researchers and practitioners in navigating the complicated world of quantitative data analysis. Our goal is to provide a foundation for developing one's mental model for quantitative analysis, as well as gaining an understanding of the various methods of quantitative analysis that are currently available. We cover the philosophical and theoretical foundations of quantitative analysis, the interconnections between data collection methods and quantitative analysis, how the nature of the data collected impacts on quantitative analysis and the steps involved with preparing data for quantitative analysis. This book covers many of the most common quantitative analyses available to researchers and practitioners in answering research or business questions. Subsequent books in this series will address many of the less common and advanced methods (e.g. factor analysis, conjoint analysis) that are not covered here.

It has been our observation that books on quantitative analysis rarely focus on the more conceptual aspects of thinking about and planning quantitative analyses. They also do not focus on the link between quantitative analyses and research design and methods. In crafting this book, we attempt to address this gap. We have striven to provide guidance on the factors that one needs to consider, the steps that one should take and the decisions that one must make when engaging in quantitative analysis. We intentionally avoid providing an inflexible rule-bound system that leads to the 'one and only' quantitative analysis that is appropriate for a given situation. As Abelson (1995) argues, there is rarely only one correct choice or rule. However, taking such an approach does involve a trade-off. The trade-off is that we focus less on providing detailed descriptions of every aspect of every quantitative analysis and the procedures for running them in statistical software programs. Given the wide availability of exceptional resources covering every single detail of quantitative analyses and using the statistical software (e.g. Cohen et al., 2003; Field, 2013; Pedhazur and Pedhazur-Schmelkin, 1991), we felt that it was a trade-off that will benefit those just starting out on the journey of using quantitative analyses.

WHAT IS QUANTITATIVE ANALYSIS?

Quantitative analysis is statistics. It is procedures and rules used to reduce large amounts of data into more manageable forms that allow one to draw conclusions and insights about patterns in the data. Although there are many types of quantitative analyses, this book focuses on common methods that are used to describe quantitative data, to identify differences between groups, to examine associations or relationships between variables, or to make predictions. The most basic form of quantitative analysis is the descriptive quantitative analysis. Descriptive quantitative analyses can be used to condense large amounts of data into a smaller set of numbers representing what is typical in the data and the amount of variability in the data. As described in Part I of Chapter 4, descriptive quantitative analyses include the frequency, mode, median and mean (type of average) as well as the range, variance and standard deviation. Descriptive quantitative analyses can be represented in both numerical and graphical forms (e.g. bar charts and histograms). Regardless of the research question or research method, descriptive quantitative analyses should always be one of the first steps in the process of analysing data.

Related to descriptive analyses are quantitative analyses that examine differences between groups on an outcome or set of outcomes. For example, these analyses might be used to examine differences in customer engagement of those who receive an individualized promotion versus those who receive a generic promotion. As described in Part II of Chapter 4, these analyses typically examine differences in means between groups and include *t*-tests and analysis of variance.

Other quantitative analyses focus on the direction and strength of relationships between variables, and, as an extension of this, aim to predict one variable based on another. These analyses are correlation and regression methods (see Part III of Chapter 4). Correlation is often a first step in understanding whether variables are related. Regression analyses extend correlations by allowing one to create an equation that can be used to predict or forecast an outcome based on a set of inputs. For example, equations could be developed that allow one to predict future employee sales performance from the current investment in sales training.

HISTORICAL FOUNDATIONS OF QUANTITATIVE ANALYSIS AND CURRENT TRENDS

Although much of the current coverage and discussion of quantitative data analysis treats it as if it is a revolutionary breakthrough that has just occurred, most of the commonly used quantitative analyses were developed over 100 years ago. Although a detailed review of the history of the development of quantitative analysis is beyond the scope of this book (see Lehman, 2011 or Salsburg, 2002 for detailed historical reviews), it is important to consider some challenges in research that led to the initial development of many of the analyses discussed in this book and that still continue to influence quantitative analysis today.

Much of the research in the business and managerial sciences is focused on questions related to large groups. For example, researchers might be interested in the effectiveness of training sales professionals in persuasion techniques for increasing sales productivity. Researchers implement the training at one company with a small group of sales professionals, collect data on the completion of the training and sales productivity, and analyse the data. Ultimately, the researchers are not interested in the specific sales professionals in their study. They are interested in all sales professionals. The question is how one can generalize their findings from the specific group of sales professionals that were part of their study to the much larger group that represents all sales professionals. More specifically, the question is how well a statistic computed from a sample (e.g. an average in the sample) is an adequate estimate of that same statistic in the population (i.e. a population parameter). This question is one that early statisticians developed methods to address. That is, are generalizations about a population justified if analyses are only based on a sample of that population? Populations represent the entire group of interest for a specific research question (e.g. the population of England). Samples represent a subset of the population (e.g. those willing to complete a survey while walking through Trafalgar Square on a given day).

The process of collecting a sample from the population involves a degree of uncertainty. The uncertainty is that a researcher does not know if his or her sample is an adequate representation of the population. It is no surprise that any given sample will not be a perfect reflection of the population. There is always some degree of error when using a sample statistic as an estimate of a population parameter, aptly named sampling error. This sampling error can lead to fluctuations in results between research studies on the same topic. The major concern with these fluctuations is that a researcher may collect data from a sample that is not truly reflective of the broad population, and then the inferences that are drawn from this sample about the population can be erroneous. One of the most well-known examples of sampling error gone awry was the 1948 presidential election in the USA. After polling a group of voters that was not representative of the voting population, the *Chicago Tribune* newspaper predicted that Thomas Dewey had defeated Harry Truman and published a headline to that effect. However, Harry Truman had a decisive victory, causing quite an embarrassment for the newspaper. Quantitative analyses were developed to assist in determining whether inferences from a sample to a population are indeed merited, especially when the sample represents a very small percentage of the population.

Practical problems in drawing inferences from a sample of data sparked much of the development of quantitative analysis. However, the current rise in the use of quantitative analysis has been fuelled by both the availability of large amounts of data from different sources that can be integrated (i.e. 'big data') and the development of quantitative analysis software (McAfee and Brynjolfsson, 2012; Mayer-Schönberger and Cukier, 2013). It was once the case that data were difficult to obtain, they were small in quantity and needed to be examined in isolation. With technological advances, large volumes of data are now available from multiple sources and can be integrated. For example, it is now possible to integrate data from point of sale transactions, customer satisfaction surveys, web traffic, customer service training completed, employee engagement, and compensation for every single sales transaction and every single employee in an organization.

Box 1.1   Big data in action

Most large retailers are currently using 'big data' from their point of sales transactions, web traffic, customer surveys and responses to marketing campaigns to tailor coupons and advertisements to customers to help increase purchase behaviours. One North American retailer used its large database of purchase history across all of its customers and its database of customers who signed up for the baby registry to predict which female customers were likely to be starting their second trimester of pregnancy. One can imagine the customers' surprise when brochures for newborn products arrived in the mail before they had even announced the pregnancy to friends and family! Although the use of data in this manner may raise ethical concerns, it is this capacity to integrate and leverage the large amount of data created by normal business operations that has exponentially increased the widespread adoption of quantitative analysis.

The availability of statistical software has substantially impacted on the rapid proliferation of quantitative analysis, particularly in business. Executing quantitative analyses was once the sole province of highly skilled experts. The software required specialized knowledge to make choices among all of the available analyses and the multitude of options that exist within each analysis. Contemporarily, a considerable amount of new software has been developed for use by non-experts. For example, IBM's SPSS Modeler offers automatic selections among the options for a particular analysis and analyses are conducted using visual schematics in which the user drags a node representing a particular class of analysis (e.g. regression) and connects it to a node representing the data. The software then does the rest. The user does not need to make any other decisions. All that is needed is the software, the data and an idea of the general type of analysis required. As will be argued throughout this book, the blind and uncritical use of quantitative analysis is not recommended and can con- tribute to the misuse of quantitative analysis, as well as have a negative impact of progress on a field's theories.

KEY CONCEPTS IN QUANTITATIVE ANALYSIS

Regardless of the specific quantitative analysis selected, there are a number of key concepts with which all users of quantitative analyses need to be familiar with. One of the most fundamental concepts in quantitative research and analysis is measurement (Scherbaum and Meade, 2009). Measurement can be conceptualized as the assign- ment of numbers to properties or attributes of objects, events or people according to a set of rules (Stevens, 1968). It is these properties or attributes of objects, events or people that serve as the variables in quantitative analyses. In much of manage- ment research, these variables are used as indirect indicators of unobservable con- structs. Constructs are abstractions developed to explain differences, commonalities or patterns in the properties or attributes of objects, events or people. For exam- ple, personality is a well-known construct that has been used in the managerial and organizational sciences. Personality is an abstraction developed by psychologists to examine differences between people in their behavioural tendencies and interactions with the environment.

Constructs form the basis of many theories in business and the management sciences. These theories, in turn, are the source of hypotheses that quantitative anal- yses are designed to test. Hypotheses are testable statements about the anticipated relationships or differences between variables in the population. Hypotheses are tested using data collected from a sample drawn from the relevant population. The results of a quantitative analysis are used to determine whether the data collected from the sample support inferences about the population. A point that will be made throughout this book is the importance of theory and hypotheses as part of the use of quantitative analyses. Although quantitative analyses can be and often are used without theory or hypotheses, we strongly discourage this practice. There are fields such as internet search analytics, market research or crime prevention where the only research questions of interest are 'what happens?' or 'do customers who buy one particular product also buy another particular product?' For these descriptive uses of quantitative analysis, theory may not be necessary. However, in much of business and management research, the research questions or hypotheses of interest focus on why some effect or phenomenon happens. These questions cannot be adequately answered without theory guiding the analyses.

As will be elaborated on in Chapter 2, a foundational concept in quantitative analysis is probability. Probability can be described as the likelihood of a particular outcome. Probabilities range from 0.00 (no chance of an outcome occurring) to 1.00 (the outcome is certain to occur). Probabilities serve as the basis for all quantitative analyses that seek to generalize from a sample to a population. Whether or not a hypothesis is considered to be supported rests on the probability associated with the observed result from a quantitative analysis. In other words, probability is one of the primary criteria used to determine whether inferences about the population are supported by the data collected from a sample.

UNDERSTANDING THE INTERPLAY BETWEEN QUANTITATIVE ANALYSIS AND RESEARCH METHODS

As elaborated on in Chapter 3, there are fundamental relationships between research methods, research design and quantitative analysis. The methods and design used in a research study impact on the nature of the conclusions drawn from quantitative analyses, the type of analysis that may be appropriate, the amount of data that is required and the likelihood that the assumptions of a particular quantitative analysis will be met. For example, non-experimental research designs will never support strong conclusions about causality, regardless of the quantitative analysis used. Likewise, if the data collected represent categories (e.g. male/female; yes/no), only a limited number of quantitative analyses is appropriate. Users of quantitative analyses need to be aware of the close relationship between research methods, research design and quantitative analysis. With that said, we do not advocate designing research to support the use of particular quantitative analyses. Theory and the research questions should determine the research design and method which in turn determine the best quantitative analysis.

Research method and design are also related to quantitative analysis in some less obvious ways. Traditions have developed in many scientific fields about the 'right' analysis for certain types of research designs. For example, quantitative data from experimental research study are more frequently analysed using analysis of variance and t-tests (see Part II of Chapter 4), while non-experimental data are more frequently analysed using correlation and regression (see Part III of Chapter 4). Although certain analyses may be more insightful for the types of research questions that are typically studied with a certain research design, there are no explicit rules stating that particular analyses are the most appropriate for particular research designs. We strongly encourage users of quantitative analyses to consider all of the analysis that may be possible in a given context, regardless of whether or not the analysis is what is typical for the selected research design.

SUMMARY

The interest in quantitative analysis has dramatically increased in recent years. Most fields of research and practice have intentionally or unintentionally made understanding, using and interpreting quantitative data analysis a core area of competence. Despite the recent surge in interest, quantitative analysis is by no means new. Many common quantitative analyses were developed long ago to deal with problems such as the uncertainty inherent in drawing inferences from a sample to a population. In this book, we describe the basis of quantitative analysis, many of the basic quantitative analyses available, how to select quantitative analyses and the major considerations in using quantitative analyses. More specifically, this book will help those using quantitative analyses to understand the philosophical underpinnings, the connections to research design and methods, the connections to the properties of the data and the major strengths and limitations of quantitative analyses. It will also provide step-by-step guidance on how to execute the primary quantitative analyses used with experimental and non-experimental research, as well as alternative analyses that can be used when the assumptions of the most common analyses are not met. Each analysis presented will include an example that the reader can use to practise manually computing the analysis using the formulas in the text, as well as computing them in Excel. All formulas for the analyses in Excel will be presented next to the results in the examples and in the Appendix. As we will emphasize throughout this book, quantitative analysis can be a powerful and very useful tool for those conducting research. However, its use requires careful thought and theory or conceptual frameworks of the problems we study. The blind use of quantitative analyses can never lead to true insight into the research questions we ask.

2

UNDERSTANDING QUANTITATIVE DATA ANALYSIS

Questions concerning the nature of reality and the creation of knowledge were once the sole province of philosophy and something that researchers rarely considered as there was a dominant and widely shared paradigm for conceptualizing scientific research. Thus, there was rarely a need for a business, organizational or management researcher to articulate their underlying assumptions about the nature of reality (e.g. objective, subjective) and how knowledge can be created. Times have changed. Research in the business, organizational and management sciences now uses a wide variety of different paradigms with vastly different assumptions about the nature of reality and how knowledge can and should be created (Buchanan and Bryman, 2009; Deetz, 1996). For example, articles drawing on epistemologies ranging from positivism to hermeneutics, realism, post-modernism and phenomenology are common in organizational and management science journals.

Although the diversity in perspectives has been beneficial for building better theories and better understanding of the phenomena that we study, it has also created some challenges. The major challenge is that to understand, design, execute and evaluate today's business, organizational and management research, one now needs a clear articulation of the ontological (i.e. what constitutes reality?) and epistemological (i.e. what are appropriate approaches to knowledge creation?) assumptions underlying the research questions, research design and quantitative analyses. Different epistemological assumptions have implications for the type of research design that is most appropriate, as well as for the type of data that can be gathered from the research design. The nature of the data can determine whether quantitative analysis is appropriate at all and, if so, which particular analyses are appropriate. Therefore, researchers need to consider the extent to which their approach to quantitative analysis is compatible with the epistemological perspective that they intend to adopt in their research.

THE ROLE OF ONTOLOGY AND EPISTEMOLOGY IN QUANTITATIVE ANALYSIS

In the context of quantitative analysis, ontology and epistemology most directly play a role in defining what are considered data, the form of the data and the nature of the conclusions that can be drawn from the data. In considering the impact of the ontological and epistemological perspective on the appropriateness of quantitative analyses, one must differentiate between descriptive and inferential quantitative analysis. The goal of descriptive quantitative analyses, as the name implies, is to quantitatively describe or summarize data. These quantitative analyses only attempt to describe a particular aspect of a set of data (e.g. an average of the set of data, variability in the data). These analyses are described in detail in Part I of Chapter 4. The goal of inferential quantitative analyses is to evaluate the viability of inferences about the generalizability of the relationships, associations or differences observed in the sample in regard to the population. Inferential quantitative analyses are the primary analytical tools that are used to evaluate research questions and hypotheses. These analyses are described in detail in Parts II, III and IV of Chapter 4. The appropriateness of either descriptive or inferential quantitative analyses, given an epistemological perspective, can be evaluated on several criteria, including the desired degree of quantification and the desired degree of generalizability.

The use of any quantitative analyses requires the measurement and quantification of observations and information. In other words, quantitative analysis requires numbers. Although all epistemological perspectives allow for some form of measurement of the phenomena of interest, only some allow for quantitative forms of measurement. Some epistemological perspectives argue that the phenomena we study are too complex to be reduced to numerical data and require a contextual interpretation that is not possible with decontextualized numbers. For example, hermeneutic perspectives focus on the interpretive understanding of phenomena over explanation and description due to the belief that phenomena are too complex for formalistic and decontextualized observation and measurement. For example, research in this tradition has the researcher as a participant and an observer who is experiencing the context as any member of the context would. This is quite the opposite of remotely sending surveys or observing from afar (e.g. watching video footage). Quantitative analyses necessitate quantification of data and are therefore not consistent with this epistemological perspective. Phenomenological perspectives, on the other hand, allow for the possibility of quantification of measurement and observation and urge that these measures and observations be gathered using multiple methods. Therefore, quantitative analyses are more compatible with this perspective. In general, epistemological perspectives that support the quantification of information, measurement and observations are compatible with descriptive quantitative analyses and, depending on the other criteria, may be compatible with inferential quantitative analyses. For the epistemological perspectives that do not support quantification, quantitative analyses are not appropriate.

As described in Chapter 1, quantitative analyses were designed in part to address the challenges of drawing inferences about a population from a sample. In other words, quantitative analyses support generalizations from a given research context to other contexts. Not all epistemological perspectives support the position that this type of generalizability is possible or should be pursued. For example, naturalistic inquiry is based on the assumption that there is no single objective reality, only multiple constructed realities. Thus, phenomena must be studied holistically and phenomena can only be understood within the specific context that they exist. In most instances, this position is not likely to be compatible with the generalizability goal of inferential quantitative analyses. Alternatively, the positivist and realist epistemologies hold that there is an objective reality; these positions argue that the purpose of science is to develop objective and generalizable facts and principles. These positions are compatible with the generalizability goal of inferential quantitative analyses. For other perspectives, such as critical realism, the possibility of generalization will depend on the nature of the data. For example, when measuring objective properties such as physical measures, sales or other properties that do not require subjective judgement, critical realism is compatible with inferential quantitative analyses. When the data are a measure of a property that requires subjective judgement (e.g. attitudes, perceptions, beliefs), it is not compatible. If the epistemological perspective supports even limited generalizations from a sample to a larger population (even if that population is limited), inferential quantitative analyses may be compatible with the perspective. However, if the perspective does not allow for sample-to-population generalizations, then inferential quantitative analyses are not appropriate, while descriptive quantitative analyses may still be appropriate.

Based on the criteria of the desired degree of quantification and the desired degree of generalizability, Table 2.1 describes the compatibility, in general, of several epistemological perspectives with descriptive and inferential quantitative analyses. This list is by no means exhaustive of the possible perspectives, but provides a sample of the types of perspectives currently in use and the appropriateness of quantitative analyses with these perspectives in general. As can be seen in this table, perspectives associated with positivism tend to be uniformly compatible with all forms of quantitative analysis, perspectives associated with interpretivism can be compatible with one or both forms of quantitative analysis, and perspectives associated with critical inquiry tend not to be compatible with quantitative analysis.

Table 2.1 Compatibility of common epistemological perspectives with quantitative analysis

Perspective	Descriptive Quantitative Analyses	Inferential Quantitative Analyses
Critical theory	Not compatible	Not compatible
Post modernism	Not compatible	Not compatible
Phenomenology	Compatible	Not compatible
Naturalistic inquiry	Not compatible	Not compatible
Symbolic interaction	Compatible	Compatible
Hermeneutics	Not compatible	Not compatible
Realism	Compatible	Compatible
Critical realism	Possibly compatible*	Possibly compatible*
Interpretivism	Compatible	Not compatible
Positivist	Compatible	Compatible
Post-positivist	Compatible	Compatible

Note: * = Compatible when measuring objective properties.

POST-POSITIVIST FOUNDATIONS OF INFERENTIAL QUANTITATIVE ANALYSIS

Although quantitative analyses are almost always viewed as the province of the positivist perspective, several epistemological perspectives are compatible with descriptive analyses (see Table 2.1). However, the process of inferential quantitative analysis is arguably aligned with only the post-positivist perspective. Thus, using inferential statistics requires one to adopt some of the tenets of this perspective. The post-positivist perspective, like the positivist perspective, is rooted in the notion of an objective reality. The study of this objective reality should be impartial and value free. Science requires verifiable measurement and observation (i.e. data). Although there are many differences between post-positivist and positivist perspectives (Popper, 1959), the most important for quantitative analyses are differences in the nature of how the truth can be obtained.

A post-positivist perspective is based on the falsification principle (Popper, 1959). This principle states that theories and hypotheses can never be proven true; they can only be proven false. The elegance of this idea is that it takes only one contrary instance to prove a theory or hypothesis false or that it is at least not unconditionally true. For example, it was once believed that all swans were white. It took a single observation of a black swan to disprove this scientific belief (Taleb, 2007). It would take a never-ending series of supporting instances to prove a rule, theory or hypothesis true, and with each new test a new uncertainty arises about whether the results will be contrary or supportive. A way to remove this uncertainty is to focus on falsification (i.e. look for the black swans, not the white ones!). Thus, the failure to reject a theory or hypothesis over many conceptual or exact replications is the only path toward tentative acceptance of a theory or hypothesis. However, the next instance could change that tentative acceptance. It is this post-positivist logic of falsification that forms the core of the null hypothesis significance testing tradition on which inferential quantitative analyses are based.

NULL HYPOTHESIS SIGNIFICANCE TESTING

Inferential quantitative analyses are designed to test hypotheses about populations. The first step in a quantitative analysis is to form a hypothesis about the population. For example, a hypothesis could state that 'organizational size is negatively associated with the degree of success of organizational change efforts, such that the degree of success decreases as the size of the organization increases'. Hypotheses are most often statements about the existence of relationships, associations or differences in populations. These hypotheses are typically what the researcher hopes to find. Given that these hypotheses cannot be proven true, only false, the quantitative analysis process starts by forming both the research hypothesis (denoted H_1 in quantitative analysis nomenclature) and its opposite – the null hypothesis (denoted H_0 in quantitative analysis nomenclature). It is important to note that in most research publications, the null hypothesis is only implied. It is rare that one will see it explicitly listed in published journal articles.

The null hypothesis is a statement that there is no relationship, no association or no difference. Thinking in quantitative terms, many null hypotheses are statements that the value of a quantitative index of a relationship, association or difference is zero. The research hypothesis is then that the value of the index is not zero. Research hypotheses can be directional (e.g. the mean scores of group 1 are greater than the mean scores of group 2) or non-directional (e.g. the mean scores of group 1 are not equal to the mean scores of group 2). The null hypothesis and research hypothesis are mutually exclusive, so they will always posit opposite relationships (e.g. the corresponding null hypotheses for the previous examples would be the mean scores of group 1 are less than or equal to the mean scores of group 2 or the mean scores of group 1 are equal to the mean scores of group 2).

Instead of attempting to falsify the research hypothesis, quantitative analyses attempt to falsify the null hypothesis. Because the null and research hypotheses are mutually exclusive, the logic follows that if the hypothesis of no relationships, no associations or no differences (the null hypothesis) is falsified, then relationships, associations or differences exist, as posited by the research hypothesis. In other words, the support for research hypotheses of relationships, associations or differences in the population is achieved indirectly by falsifying the notion that they do not exist. In quantitative terms, one is attempting to falsify the null hypothesis that the value of an index of a relationship, association or difference is zero. If it is falsified that the index is zero, it must be significantly greater or less than zero which would demonstrate that a relationship, association or difference exists. This process of creating and testing the null and research hypothesis is carried out for all inferential quantitative analyses, although the form of the hypothesis changes according to the type of quantitative analysis.

Determination of whether the null hypothesis is false and should be rejected is made primarily using probabilities. Each inferential quantitative analysis involves computing the probability of obtaining the observed results *if* the null hypothesis is true. The probabilities are computed using a distribution of possible values of the given quantitative analysis *if* null hypothesis is true (called a sampling distribution). Each possible value in the sampling distribution can be used to determine the probability of that value (or a larger value) occurring in the sampling distribution. Large probabilities (e.g. 0.78) indicate that obtaining the observed results is likely if the null hypothesis is true. Small probabilities (e.g. .05) indicate that obtaining the observed results is unlikely *if* the null hypothesis is true. If the probability is small enough, it leads us to conclude that the null hypothesis is not true given the observed results. If the null hypothesis is rejected, the research hypothesis achieves indirect support.

The question becomes how small does a probability need to be in order to reject the null hypothesis. The current convention is to set the threshold for rejecting a null hypothesis at a probability of .05 or less (i.e. $p < .05$; Cohen, 1994). This threshold is often called the statistical significance level and is represented by the symbol α and called alpha. For example, if the probability associated with obtaining a given result from a quantitative analysis was $p = .04$, the null hypothesis would be rejected. Another way of saying that the null hypothesis is rejected is to say that the results are statistically significant. However, if the probability was $p = .06$, one would fail to reject the null hypothesis because the likelihood of the null hypothesis being true is too high (i.e. above the predetermined threshold). It is important to note that one never accepts the null hypothesis. That would be equivalent to stating that it is true. One can only reject the null hypothesis or fail to reject it. Before the wide accessibility of statistical software to compute the exact probability of a test result, the value in the sampling distribution that is associated with a probability of .05 was used to determine whether the observed result from a quantitative analysis was sufficient for rejecting the null hypothesis. The values from the sampling distribution that serve as the threshold for rejecting the null hypothesis are called critical values.

Hypotheses are statements about the population that are tested using data from a sample. Whether the null hypothesis is ultimately true or false in the population cannot be known. Thus, there is a degree of uncertainty in the accuracy of our inference about the null hypothesis. One could make the mistake of rejecting the null hypothesis when it is true in the population based on a sample. For example, we could conclude that age and purchase behaviour are related when in reality they are not. This type of incorrect decision about the null hypothesis is called a *Type I error*. *Type I errors* can occur for a number of reasons including small samples or samples that are extreme but reflect a true null hypothesis. The use of probabilities as part of the null hypothesis significance testing is an attempt to quantify and minimize the likelihood of incorrectly rejecting the null hypothesis. Using $p < .05$ as the threshold for rejecting the null hypothesis sets the probability of a *Type I error* at 5% or less. Even at this probability, a *Type I error* is possible, but the process is structured so that chances are small. If the consequences of making a *Type I error* are considerable, the researcher should consider lowering the threshold for rejecting the null hypothesis (e.g. $p < .01$).

We could also make the mistake of failing to reject the null hypothesis when it is false in the population. For example, we could conclude that age and purchase behaviour are not related when in reality they are. This type of incorrect decision about the null hypothesis is called a *Type II error* and is represented with the symbol β and called beta. *Type II errors* can occur for a number of reasons including small samples and relationships, associations or differences that are small in magnitude. This type of error has traditionally received less attention from researchers (Cohen, 1988). It can be thought of as a missed opportunity. The probability of this type of error is not set to a fixed value in the same way as a *Type I error*. It is desired that the probability of a *Type II error* be .20 or less. However, it is often far higher in business, organizational and management research (Cashen and Geiger, 2004; Combs, 2010). As is discussed in more detail in Chapter 3, $1-\beta$ is call statistical power. It is the probability of correctly rejecting a false null hypothesis (i.e. finding a relationship, association or difference when it does exist). To the degree possible, researchers want to achieve high levels of statistical power. The relationship between *Type I errors*, *Type II errors* and correct decisions about the null hypothesis are presented in Table 2.2.

Table 2.2 Relationships between Type I error, Type II error and correct decisions about the null hypothesis

	Null Hypothesis is True	Null Hypothesis is False
Reject the Null Hypothesis	Type I error α	Correct decision (statistical power) $1-\beta$
Fail to Reject the Null Hypothesis	Correct decision $1-\alpha$	Type II error β

Box 2.1 Making *Type I* and *Type II* errors

Felicity is a behavioural economics researcher who is interested in understanding how losing money may make individuals less risk seeking. Based on theory from economics and psychology, Felicity hypothesizes that individuals who lose money

(Continued)

(Continued)

will become more risk seeking than those who do not lose money. She conducts a study using a gambling task in which half the participants lose money and the other half do not lose money. In the study, Felicity examines the effects of losing money on making risky bets in the gambling task. After collecting and analysing the data, she needs to come to a conclusion about the support of her hypothesis. In making her decision, she considers the four possible outcomes:

1   The null hypothesis that losing money does not affect risk taking is true. If she rejects the null hypothesis in this case, it is an incorrect decision (α) and a *Type I error*.
2   The null hypothesis that losing money does not affect risk taking is true. If she fails to reject the null hypothesis in this case, it is a correct decision ($1-\alpha$).
3   The null hypothesis that losing money does not affect risk taking is false. If she rejects the null hypothesis in this case, it is a correct decision ($1-\beta$).
4   The null hypothesis that losing money does not affect risk taking is false. If she fails to reject the null hypothesis in this case, it is an incorrect decision (β) and a *Type II error*.

Given that the truth of the null hypothesis cannot be known, Felicity will never know for certain if her decision is correct or incorrect. She can only minimize the probability of it being incorrect by attempting to minimize the *Type I* and *Type II error* rates.

The directionality of the hypothesis does have an impact on the value of a quantitative analysis that is needed to reach a probability of less than .05. When hypotheses are directional, they should be tested using one-tailed tests. When hypotheses are non-directional, they should be tested using two-tailed tests. The general rule is that it is more likely that one will achieve a probability of .05 or less for a directional hypothesis test than for a non-directional test. That is, two-tailed tests are more conservative than one-tailed tests. In practice, two-tailed tests are typically used.

It is important to consider that the use of null hypothesis significance testing has been criticized (e.g. Kline, 2004; Schmidt and Hunter, 1997) and has clearly been abused (e.g. Frick, 1996). Some of the criticisms call for its outright abandonment (Carver, 1993; Ziliak and McCloskey, 2008), while other criticisms focus on some specific practices in the process such as the uncritical use and understanding of *Type I errors* (Abelson, 1995, 1997; Cohen, 1994) or the use of zero as the value expected under the null hypothesis (Meehl, 1978, 1990). Many of these criticisms reflect unresolved debates between the founders of modern statistics (e.g. compare the methods described by Ronald Fisher versus Jerzy Neyman and Egon Pearson; Salsburg, 2002).

These criticisms should be incorporated in the mental model of any researcher who uses quantitative analyses (Edwards, 2008). In particular, researchers need to be acutely aware that decisions about rejecting or failing to reject a null hypothesis are influenced by many factors that have no connection to the veracity of the theory or hypothesis. For example, the magnitude of effect that is needed to achieve a probability of $p < .05$ decreases as the sample size increases. In other words, it is easier to reject the null hypothesis with large samples. Likewise, it is easier to reject a null hypothesis when the null hypothesized effect is zero than when it takes on a non-zero value. However, setting non-zero values requires stronger theory than that currently normative in business, organizational and management research (Edwards and Berry, 2010). Researchers using quantitative analyses are well advised to thoroughly consider the uses and limits of null hypothesis significance tests (see Harlow et al., 1997 or Shrout, 1997 for detailed discussions on the uses and criticisms).

Regardless of where one stands on these debates, it is clear that null hypothesis significance testing can provide insights when used appropriately (Abelson, 1995; Cortina and Landis, 2011; Frick, 1996). However, it should be only one of the pieces of information used in evaluating research hypotheses. As is stressed throughout this book, a researcher should use multiple sources of information (e.g. replications, effect sizes, estimates, confidence intervals) when evaluating the adequacy of theory and hypothesis. It is becoming the case that the scientific community has an increased reliance on multiple studies replicating a finding and the use of effect sizes (see Chapter 3) as a pre-requisite for publication in academic journals.

SUMMARY

In summary, quantitative analyses start by the researcher determining whether quantitative analyses are compatible with their ontological and epistemological position and, if so, which forms of quantitative analysis are compatible (see Table 2.1). If inferential quantitative analyses are appropriate, a researcher begins the null hypothesis significance testing process. This process is based on the falsification principle that hypotheses are only proven false and never proven true, and starts with the articulation of a research and a null hypothesis as well as setting a *Type I error* rate (including the number of tails to the test). Inferential quantitative analyses are then carried out to test the null hypothesis. The researcher makes a decision regarding rejecting or failing to reject the null hypothesis based on the probabilities associated with the obtained results if the null hypothesis is true. If the probability is small enough (e.g. $p < .05$), the researcher rejects the null hypothesis. Otherwise, the researcher fails to reject the null hypothesis.

Although the null hypothesis significance testing process can be very useful, it can also be inappropriately applied (as many critics have pointed out). It is one piece of information that can be used to support or fail to support a study's research question. Decisions about the null hypothesis can be influenced by many factors that have no connection to the veracity of the theory or hypothesis. As discussed in the next chapter, researchers should carefully consider their *Type I error* rate, statistical power, effect sizes and research design when drawing conclusions from their quantitative analyses of the null hypothesis.

3

BASIC COMPONENTS OF QUANTITATIVE DATA ANALYSIS

The basic components of all quantitative analyses are research questions, hypotheses and data. In this chapter, the basic components of the data collection aspect and its implications for quantitative analysis are considered. There are a variety of different strategies that can be used to gather the data needed for the analyses. With each strategy, there are many factors that must be considered in determining the most fitting way to obtain the data. These factors and the choices about them have considerable implications for the quantitative analyses and the conclusions drawn from them (Aguinis and Vandenberg, 2014). In considering the interplay between methods and analysis, Sir Ronald Fisher is famous for concluding, '[t]o consult the statistician after an experiment is finished is often merely to ask him to conduct a post mortem examination. He can perhaps say what the experiment died of' (Fisher, 1938: 17). Choices about method and analysis are not separable and should be considered together.

In addition to research design choices, two important additional basic components are the determination of the sample size needed for adequate tests of the study's hypotheses and the method for identifying and selecting the sample. These basic components are highly interrelated with the research design and the quantitative analyses (Austin et al., 1998; Kalton, 1983). They are ultimately questions about the statistical power of the quantitative analyses, the representativeness of the results for the intended population and the generalizability of the results. The success of the quantitative analyses and the interpretation of the results of quantitative analyses often depend on the choices a researcher makes about these basic components. All users of quantitative analyses are well advised to incorporate considerations of research design, measurement, statistical power and sampling into their mental model of the quantitative analysis process.

In order to provide guidance on making choices about these basic components, this chapter covers some basic terminology and approaches to research design and measurement, determining the required sample sizes, sampling methods and the implication of these choices for the quantitative analysis of the data. This chapter consists of two parts. The first part considers the relationships between measurement, research design and quantitative analyses. The second part considers the relationships between sample sizes, sampling methods and quantitative analyses.

PART I: MEASUREMENT, RESEARCH DESIGN AND QUANTITATIVE ANALYSES

Defining and operationalizing variables

Quantitative data analysis requires that researchers investigate at least one, but typically two or more, variables. As mentioned in Chapter 1, variables are properties or attributes of objects, events or people that can take on different values. Commonly studied business variables include number of units sold, production methods, level of job satisfaction, strategy employed, customer engagement, return on investment and gender. If a certain variable of interest demonstrates the same value across all instances within a set of data, then it is not a variable (it does not vary!) and cannot be analysed other than simply reporting its value. For example, if we are interested in studying the relationship between industry and labour strategy, but the sample consists only of companies from the technology industry, the question cannot be addressed as there is no variability in industry and there is no comparative group (i.e. retail, manufacturing, financial services) in the sample.

Variables can be further distinguished based on their role in a study. In studies that use experimental or quasi-experimental designs (described in the next section), at least one variable serves as an independent variable and at least one variable serves as a dependent variable. The independent variable is manipulated by the researcher. This variable is thought of as the 'cause'. It will have at least two levels or conditions (e.g. intervention versus no intervention conditions). As the name implies, the dependent variable depends on the level of independent variable. After individuals in a research study are exposed to the independent variable, the dependent variable is measured. Consider this variable the 'effect'. In non-experiments, slightly different terminology is used, including the term predictor for the independent variable and criterion for the dependent variable.

Box 3.1   Operationalizing independent and dependent variables

Jay is a training and development specialist who needs to make a decision about whether to implement an online or in-person training program for increasing the IT knowledge of employees. To conduct this study, half of the employees in the organization receive the in-person training and the other half receive the online training. One week after undergoing the training, these employees are given an IT knowledge test. The independent variable, the one that the researcher manipulated, is the type of training program. The two levels of the independent variable are the in-person and the online training. The dependent variable, the variable measured after administering the independent variable, is the score on the IT knowledge test. If one of the training programs is more effective, we would expect there to be a statistically significant difference in the scores from the IT knowledge test given after the training across the two groups.

Operationalization of variables within a research study

When crafting hypotheses, variables are stated in abstract terms. When using data and quantitative analyses to test the hypotheses, researchers must carefully consider how to operationalize, or turn into measurable form, these abstract ideas. When dealing with a manipulated independent variable, operationalization is often straightforward. For example, if a hypothesis proposes that customers that receive individualized coupons will report greater purchase intentions, the two levels of the independent variable are operationalized as simply receiving or not receiving the individualized coupon. Similarly, in the study in Box 3.1 aimed at comparing the effect of an online or in-person training program on IT knowledge, the independent variable would be operationalized as the administration of an online training program or an in-person training program.

Typically, the variable that requires greater thoughtfulness in operationalization is the measured variable(s) - the dependent variable in experimental research and both variables in non-experimental research. Drawing from the above examples, in order to assess the hypothesis, the theoretical constructs of purchase intentions and IT knowledge, which serve as the dependent variable, must be captured in some tangible and quantitative way. The measure must also actually reflect the construct that it is intended to measure. Said otherwise, the researcher must create some sort of assessment that can produce numerical values that represent an individual's level of purchase intentions or IT knowledge. The operationalization of an individual's perceptions, attitudes and cognitions is typically more complex than the operationalization of objective variables such as number of mobile phones sold, salary or stock performance.

A full discussion of the measurement of subjective constructs is beyond the scope of this book (see Scherbaum and Meade, 2009, 2013 for reviews), but a couple of points are important to note. Measures of perceptions, attitudes and cognitions most commonly use multiple questions or multiple items to create measures or scales, as they are commonly referred to. Consider the case of a need for affiliation at work, defined as a desire to be near, cooperate and engage in reciprocal relationships with others in the workplace context (Murray, 1938). This definition of need for achievement at work encompasses numerous facets (being near others, cooperating with others and engaging in reciprocal relationships with others), which would be difficult to capture in a single question and thus would be better captured in a multi-item scale. This is in fact what previous researchers have done when measuring it. As an example, see Table 3.1 for the items used to measure need for affiliation at work in Shockley and Allen (2010). These multiple items are ultimately combined to create an overall score for each respondent on need for affiliation at work (see Part I of Chapter 4).

Table 3.1   Need for affiliation at work items

Please indicate your agreement with the following statements. Response options include strongly disagree, disagree, neither disagree nor agree, agree, and strongly agree.

1.   I spend a lot of time talking to co-workers during work.
2.   It is important for me to feel like I am part of a work community.
3.   I am concerned with the well-being of my co-workers.
4.   I like to feel that I have meaningful relationships with my co-workers.
5.   At work, I am most content when surrounded by others.
6.   I prefer to work alone than with others.[R]
7.   I don't feel the need to gain the acceptance and approval of my co-workers. [R]

Note: [R] indicates that the item is reverse scored.
Source: Shockley and Allen (2010). Copyright 2010, with permission from Elsevier.

Scales of numerical measurement

Researchers can capture measured variables through a variety of methods. The first consideration is the scale of numerical measurement, which has implications for the quantitative analyses that can ultimately be conducted. Scales of numerical measurement (Stevens, 1968) reflect the qualities of the numbers that are assigned to the properties or attributes of objects, events or people. There are four scales of measure: nominal, ordinal, interval and ratio.

Nominal means 'name', and nominal scales include distinct categories that have no inherent numerical value. As an example, colour preference is typically measured using a nominal scale. Blue, green, red and yellow are all different types of colours, but they each have distinct meaning. If a number was assigned to yellow it would not represent a larger value of colour than a number assigned to blue – no such idea exists with these categories. Nominal scales should be used when the only way to meaningfully measure a variable is by categories. This type of measurement scale is often applied in business and management research. For example, studies often examine industry, customer segment, sales channel or geography as variables. The quantitative analyses that are possible are more limited when the dependent variable is on a nominal scale of measurement.

Ordinal scales can be thought of as capturing rank order. For example, the finishing place in a marathon (1st, 2nd, 3rd, etc.) is an ordinal variable. While this scale of measurement does incorporate inherent value (1st is meaningfully faster than 2nd), it is limited in that the distance between values is unknown and is not fixed. The person who came in 1st place may have beaten the person in 2nd place by 1 second, but the person in 2nd place may have beaten the person in 3rd place by 2 minutes. The lack of consistency in the distance between numbers creates difficulties for using ordinal scales of measurement for many common quantitative analyses. When possible, the information used to calculate the rank order (i.e. finishing time in minutes) should be used instead as it allows for a greater number of possible quantitative analyses. Ordinal scales are used in business and management research but are not particularly common.

Like ordinal scales, interval scales of measurement also have inherent value. They differ in that the distance between any two units of measurement is equivalent. However, interval scales do not contain a true zero, meaning that zero represents the complete absence of the construct. A common example of an interval scale is temperature. When a thermometer reads 0 degrees Celsius, this does not mean the absence of a temperature. It is just very cold. It does imply that 10 degrees Celsius is one degree colder than 11 degrees Celsius. In business and management research, interval scales are common. The majority of variables related to customer and employee experiences, opinions and characteristics (e.g. personality) are on an interval scale.

Finally, ratio scales have meaningful values, a constant distance between any two units, and incorporate a true zero point. An example is the number of mobile phones manufactured (zero indicates that none were manufactured). Ratio scales are commonly used with variables that involve a count or an amount (e.g. behaviours, number of items sold, transactions or errors). These scales are common in business and management research and allow for many different quantitative analyses.

Implications of the measurement of variables for quantitative analysis

As will be reiterated throughout this book, we urge researchers to consider the operationalization and measurement of variables in conjunction with the ultimate goal of the research. The way variables are conceptualized has a direct impact on the type of conclusions that can be drawn. Consider the example above with the need for affiliation. In Shockley and Allen's (2010) study, it was measured via a survey with an interval scale of measurement. However, one could conceivably also measure need for affiliation via a ratio scale by using sociometric badges. These are wearable devices that use an infrared transceiver, a microphone and accelometers to record movement, speech patterns and detection of others in close proximity. These data, particularly those that involve interactions with others, could be used as an indicator of need for affiliation. We would expect those with higher needs for affiliation to spend more time with others relative to those with lower needs. Because these types of data include a true zero, it represents a ratio scale of measurement. Likewise, one could observe individuals interacting and rank them according to the level of interactions with others as an indicator of need for affiliation. Because these types of data are ranks, it represents an ordinal scale of measurement. With each operationalization, different quantitative analyses may be selected to best use the properties of the data.

As a final note, it is generally advisable for researchers to use interval and ratio measurement scales when it is feasible given the research question. These scales allow for the computation of means and standard deviations, which allow the use of more powerful inferential quantitative analyses. Researchers will be quite limited in the quantitative analyses that can be conducted if nominal or ordinal scales of measurement are used.

Research designs

There are many variations on research study design, but these can be categorized into three broad types that are relevant as a basic component for quantitative analyses: experimental, quasi-experimental and non-experimental designs.

Experimental designs

People commonly label any research study an experiment. However, a 'true' randomized experiment requires that three conditions be met: (1) there must be an independent variable that is manipulated by the researcher; (2) there must be a dependent variable that is assessed after participants are exposed to the independent variable; and (3) if employing a between-subjects design, participants must be randomly assigned to the various levels of the independent variable. For random assignment to occur, the researcher must use a system that allows for an equal chance of each research participant being assigned to any condition of the independent variable. Randomly assigning individuals to conditions can be done using random number tables or random number generators that are included in most statistical software.

Box 3.2   Random assignment in action

Yasmin is a market researcher at a South American hypermarket who is interested in determining the most effective layout of email coupons to encourage customers to click an offer to learn more about a product and make a purchase. To examine the effectiveness of different possible layouts, she knows that a randomized experiment will be the best research design which will involve assigning customers to receive different layouts of the coupons. Several of her colleagues in the market research department suggest that she should allow the customers to choose which coupon layout they receive. Yasmin argues that if customers are allowed to choose, the assignment would not be random and the research design would no longer be a randomized experiment. She uses a random number generator to assign the customers to one of four possible layouts. She then examines whether there are different click-through rates and purchases between the four possible layouts.

A between-subjects design refers to the fact that a different group of participants partake in each condition in the study and necessitates random assignment to be deemed a 'true' experiment. When conducting a within-subjects experiment, random assignment is not necessary. This is because a within-subjects study design involves the same group of participants being exposed sequentially to all conditions of the independent variable. In addition to requiring a smaller sample size, a main advantage of a within-subjects design is that it reduces the variance associated with individual differences of participants (i.e. individual differences on the dependent variable at the start of the research study). Through random assignment, we expect these individual differences, on average, to be the same across conditions, but in a within-subjects design this is necessarily the case. Within-subject designs also have drawbacks, mainly due to the threat of carry-over effects occurring, such as when participants are exposed to one condition, they perform differently during exposure to the second condition because of familiarity or fatigue. To address this issue, researchers often randomly counter-balance the order of the conditions to which different participants are exposed.

Quasi-experimental designs

Quasi-experiments resemble experiments in many ways. They require the inclusion of an independent variable and a dependent variable that is assessed after participants are exposed to the independent variable. The differentiating factor is that in between-subject quasi-experiments participants are not randomly assigned to conditions. Hence, they are often called non-randomized experiments. In many cases, quasi-experimental designs may not be preferable for reasons discussed in the next sections, though they are sometimes inevitable. Logistics, costs, ethical concerns or perceptions of fairness, among other things, may prohibit random assignment. For example, an organization may want to conduct a study on the efficacy of flexible work arrangements in reducing employees' work-life conflict. But if they randomly allow some employees to use the flexible work arrangements and others not, feelings of injustice may arise. Instead, the organization may decide to unveil the program to employees working in Brussels, but not to those working in New York. Perceptions of unfairness may still arise but would be less likely.

In other circumstances, the independent variable is naturally occurring, meaning that it is not manipulated by the researcher. Although quasi-experiments have an independent variable and a dependent variable, the lack of random assignment or the ability to manipulate the independent variable precludes firm assumptions and conclusions about causality, as we will discuss.

Box 3.3   Quasi-experiments in action

Wagner, Barnes, Lim and Ferris (2012) were interested in the effects of daylight savings time (i.e. summer time) on cyberloafing (e.g. spending work time and using company internet access for personal reasons not related to work). On the Monday after daylight savings time, the researchers compared the internet search behaviours of employees in locations in the USA that participate in daylight savings time to those in locations that do not participate in it. In this case, the researchers could not randomly assign participants to the two levels of the independent variable (whether they experienced daylight savings time or not) and were thus limited to where participants naturally lived. Therefore, the research employed a quasi-experimental design as the independent variable was not manipulated and participants were not assigned to conditions.

Non-experimental designs

Non-experimental studies do not involve a true independent or dependent variable, and nothing is manipulated by the researcher. The goal of non-experimental studies is to simply understand if two variables are related or associated – cause and effect cannot be inferred. Non-experimental studies may involve survey measures, objective data (e.g. firm performance or stock price) or behavioural indicators. Non-experimental studies are very common in business and management research. For example, a firm may administer an annual employee survey that asks questions about a variety of constructs, such as overall job satisfaction, satisfaction with one's manager, commitment to the organization and turnover intentions. The firm could then use these data to see which variables are significantly related to turnover. Another example of a non-experimental study was published by Baughn, Neupert and Sugheir (2013), who examined the relationship between new business creation and the migration of immigrants. It is critical to keep in mind that the only appropriate statements that can be made in a non-experimental design are statements about relationships (e.g. those who are less satisfied tend to have higher desires to leave; locations with more immigrants tend to have more new businesses). Non-experimental studies may reveal a positive relationship or association or a negative (i.e. inverse) relationship or association.

Primary versus secondary data sources

Another consideration in research design is the source of the data. The description of the various research designs in the previous section assumes that the researcher is implementing the design and collecting data for analysis. However, instead of conducting a study him or herself, a researcher could use data that were originally collected for some other purpose. The former is labelled primary data and the latter is called secondary or archival data.

The choice of whether to use primary or secondary data depends on the specific research question. With experimental and quasi-experimental designs, researchers are often interested in a very specific question for which a previous experiment that addressed the question is not likely to exist. If the data already exists, the researcher may simply want to rely on those study results rather than replicating the study, unless there is a compelling reason to do so (e.g. clear flaws in the study design, a desire to replicate the study with a different sample).

Non-experimental studies tend to be more conducive to the use of secondary data. According to Hox and Boeije (2005), some reasons to use secondary data are for comparative research or replication, reanalysing the data to answer previously unanswered questions, when statistics have advanced since previous analysis or for teaching and learning purposes. Numerous data sets exist that are publicly available from data archives and government websites and include questions about phenomena relevant to business and management research. Some examples include the European Social Survey, the Panel Study of Income Dynamics, the Cornell Institute for Social and Economic Research, and the Survey of Health, Ageing and Retirement in Europe. These data sets often include nationally representative samples, and some charge fees for use, but others are open access. Other types of secondary data may be organization-specific (e.g. production records, compensation records) or general (e.g. stock market performance). In deciding if a secondary data source is fitting for a research question, it is important to closely review the sampling strategy, data collection details and variables included in the data and how they are measured to determine if they align with the research goals of the investigation at hand. It is also important to examine the codebook that is typically included with the secondary data to ensure that it provides sufficient instructions and information. The advantage of using secondary data is that it is much less costly and time-consuming, as the data are already collected. A main disadvantage is that because the data are already collected, the researcher has no say in shaping the types of variables included or the specific sample used.

Implications of research design and methods for quantitative analysis

The study design and source of data have important implications for the quantitative analyses that are appropriate for testing hypotheses and for the nature of the conclusions that can be drawn from the hypothesis testing. As described in more detail in Chapter 4, there are traditions that associate certain study designs with certain quantitative analyses. Hypotheses from experimental and quasi-experimental designs are often tested with analyses that assess mean differences (e.g. t-tests or analysis of variance). Hypotheses from non-experimental designs are often tested with analyses capturing relationships (e.g. correlations or regression). However, there is no quantitative analysis that is necessarily associated with a given study design. It ultimately depends on the specific focus of the hypotheses.

One of the major implications of research design is the nature of the conclusions that can be drawn from the data. Ultimately, the goal of much of the research in business and management is to explain patterns of relationships or differences. Inherent in this concept is that of causality - the ability to say with great confidence that one factor causes a change in another factor. It is imperative to understand that no quantitative analysis automatically allows for inferences about causality to be drawn from the data. Even when terms used in the analysis are framed in causal language (e.g. predictor or criterion), causal inferences are not assured. Whether causal inferences can be drawn is based on three conditions, which stem from the way the study is designed and carried out.

The three conditions that must be met to infer causality are: (1) the independent variable (the 'cause') must relate to the dependent variable (the 'effect'); (2) the independent variable (the 'cause') must temporally precede the dependent variable (the 'effect'); and (3) all other explanations for the relationship between the independent and dependent variables ('cause' and 'effect') can be ruled out. The first two conditions are straightforward. First, the independent and dependent variables must relate. If two variables show no association, there can simply be no causal relationship between them. The determination of association is made through statistical tests which are discussed in detail in Chapter 4 and can be calculated within the context of any of the study designs discussed above (experiments, quasi-experiments or non-experimental studies, using primary or secondary data).

The second condition requires temporal precedence of the cause before the effect. If your performance was low on Monday, several of your colleagues were unexpectedly laid off on Tuesday and then on Wednesday you blamed Monday's poor performance on the layoffs, your manager would look at you curiously. How could something you did not know about cause your poor performance the day before? For one factor to set another in motion, it simply must occur first. This condition can easily be met in study designs where the independent variable is manipulated by the researcher (experiments and some quasi-experiments). If the independent variable is first manipulated and various groups of participants within the study are exposed to the different manipulations, and then the dependent variable is subsequently measured, temporal precedence has been established.

This condition can typically not be met in non-experimental designs that are not conducted over time (as is common in business and management research). Take, for example, the common question of an increase in corporate reputation causing an increase in stock price. If we address this question by giving stock analysts a survey that asks about corporate reputation of various companies and then correlating those scores with the stock prices of those companies on the same day, we can establish a relationship between the variables (condition 1). However, we cannot be sure which variable came first and caused the other because we measured them at the same time. It is very plausible that it was stock price that caused the increase in corporate reputation rather than the reverse. Even if the researcher used two separate points in time, where corporate reputation was measured in January and stock price in June, it is still not possible to completely demonstrate time precedence. Just because you measured a variable first does not mean that it actually occurred first – it simply means that you captured it earlier in time. The differentiating factor with an experiment is that the researcher is creating the variable and in doing so has a clear sense of when it began. Thus, because the second condition cannot be met within a non-experimental design, it is incorrect to use causal language when interpreting the results of studies of this nature. It is important to note that there are some advanced longitudinal non-experimental designs that can shed some light on issues of temporal precedence, but discussion of those designs is beyond the scope of this book (see Menard, 2008 for a discussion of these methods).

The third condition of causality is the most difficult to establish. In order to conclusively say that the independent variable caused the change in the dependent variable, one must rule out the influence of all other potential causes. This is where the issue of experimental control is critical. The easiest way to rule out other causes is to make sure that none were present. That is, the best designs make sure that *everything* is equal between the groups except for the exposure to the independent variable.

Random assignment of participants into conditions of the independent variable is an important part of this process. By randomly assigning participants into groups, we hope that we have 'evened out' all the differences between individuals that might affect the dependent variable across the groups. For example, if we are assessing the efficacy of two different marketing campaigns, we would not want the group exposed to campaign A to be made up of people who already purchase the advertised product and the group exposed to marketing campaign B to be made up of people who have not previously purchased the advertised product. If this is the case, and the groups are unequal on meaningful variables, we might draw erroneous conclusions. If our quantitative analysis suggests that marketing campaign B was more efficacious, we cannot be sure that it is actually because of campaign B. It could be because the people who were exposed to campaign B were more likely to change their purchase behaviour in favour of the product (given they do not purchase it already). With random assignment, it is unlikely that this will be the case – we should have participants evenly distributed across groups so that any individual differences remaining are roughly equal between the groups. When random assignment does not take place, we cannot assume that the groups are equal and, thus, we cannot rule out other causes as an explanation for cause–effect relationships.

Other factors are also important in maintaining control. Factors such as the temperature of the room, the disposition of the researcher, the time of day, etc. should be held constant across groups. This will ensure that these factors, in addition to the independent variable, do not also influence the dependent variable differentially across levels of the independent variable. Maintaining control and complete consistency across levels of the independent variable is a major challenge in conducting research, especially because it is often difficult to foreshadow all of the variables that could potentially differ. This is more easily attained in laboratory settings than field settings, as it is impossible for the researcher to control everything in natural or field settings. The trade-off is that laboratory settings may be too artificial and not represent the way things occur in the 'real world'. In summary, only when conducting a randomized experiment with a manipulated independent variable and random assignment to groups can we infer cause and effect relationships.

Beyond its implications for causality, the concept of control within a study also has implications for the type of quantitative analysis chosen. Tests of mean differences (t-tests and analysis of variance) are conceptually based on the idea of comparing the differences between groups (participants exposed to different levels of the independent variable) to the differences within groups (natural variations across participants within each level of the independent variable). In a very controlled environment, the researcher is able to minimize the variability within groups by ensuring that each participant within each group is exposed to exactly the same conditions. This is unlikely to be the case in less controlled environments (e.g. field studies or some quasi-experiments). By minimizing this variability within groups, the researcher is facilitating the likelihood that the result of the quantitative analysis will be large, which makes the rejection of the null hypothesis more likely (these ideas are discussed in more detail in Chapter 4). As the quote from Ronald Fisher presented at the beginning of the chapter illustrates, a researcher should design his or her study with some consideration of the intended quantitative analysis.

However, the quantitative analysis should be chosen based on the research question of interest (and not the other way around).

As a final point, the decision to use primary versus secondary data also impacts quantitative analyses. When deciding whether to use available secondary data or collect new data, the researcher should consider the measurement of variables in the secondary study. As described above, the measurement of variables is a major factor in deciding which quantitative analysis is most appropriate. Even if the variables are operationalized in a way that is consistent with the researcher's goals, these goals may be thwarted by the use of certain numerical measurement scales. Furthermore, a major difference in primary versus secondary data is the task of cleaning and preparing the data for analysis (see Part I of Chapter 4). This is typically less time-consuming with primary data when the researcher has control over how the data are organized. Secondary data sets are often large, use complex coding systems and are generally difficult to navigate. This often results in considerable time spent preparing the data for a form that is usable for quantitative analysis.

Part I summary

In summary, there are a number of basic components related to obtaining data for quantitative analyses. One is whether the data are obtained from a primary source (i.e. the researcher will collect the data specifically for the research question at hand) or from a secondary source (previously collected data). In the context of the primary data strategy, the researcher has numerous decisions to make, including the design of the study (experimental, quasi-experimental or non-experimental) and the operationalization and measurement of variables. It is important to consider the nature of the research question and type of desired conclusions in choosing a study design, keeping in mind that firm assertions of causality can only be made in the case of an experiment. Moreover, the operationalization and measurement of quantitative variables are directly tied to the validity of the research as a whole and to the type of quantitative analyses that can be used to examine the data. Researchers need to carefully attend to the scale of numerical measurement of their quantitative variables as these will directly influence the appropriate quantitative analyses.

PART II: SAMPLE SIZE, SAMPLING METHODS AND QUANTITATIVE ANALYSIS

Determining required sample sizes and statistical power

When planning a research study, one of the first decisions to make is a determination of the necessary sample size. Namely, a researcher must estimate the sample size needed to achieve an acceptable level of statistical power for the quantitative analyses. Statistical power is the probability of correctly rejecting a false null hypothesis $(1-\beta)$. In other words, power is the likelihood of finding an effect if an effect actually does exist. For example, if power was equal to 0.50, the researcher has a 50% chance of rejecting the null hypothesis when it should be rejected. Ideally, one would like power to be close to 1.0, but a general rule of thumb is that the estimated level of power should be greater than 0.80 (Cohen, 1988). However, it is often well below that in business and management research (Cashen and Geiger, 2004; Combs, 2010).

Each quantitative analysis has a unique formula to estimate power (see Cohen, 1988 or Murphy and Myors, 1998 for a detailed review of statistical power formulas). In general, however, these formulas consist of four elements. The first element is power. The second element is the probability of a *Type I error* (α), which is determined by the researcher. As discussed in Chapter 2, a *Type I error* is the probability of incorrectly rejecting a true null hypothesis. That is, it is the likelihood of erroneously finding an effect when the effect does not actually exist. The third element is the effect size (*ES*). The effect size is a measure of the magnitude of the effect. Effect sizes are often standardized so that they can be interpreted as standard deviations or the percentage of the total variation explained by the effect. The fourth element is sample size (*n*), that is, how many individuals are needed to participate in the research. If the values for three of the elements are held constant (e.g. power,α and *ES*), one can estimate the value of the fourth element (i.e. sample size).

Statistical power can be estimated before or after a research study has been conducted. Conducting a power analysis after the research has been completed can be useful when a study fails to find statistically significant results. These analyses can determine whether low statistical power contributed to the lack of statistical significance. However, statistical power analyses are most useful when conducted before a research study has begun in order to determine the necessary sample size to achieve a certain level of power. It is important to keep in mind that a priori sample size requirements and statistical power are simply estimates. These estimates are based on assumptions (e.g. population parameters) that may or may not hold true (Parker and Berman, 2003). Therefore, the actual statistical power may be higher or lower than the estimated value, and more or fewer participants may be needed when the study is carried out.

There are a large number of statistical power tables and statistical calculators available in statistics books, statistical software or online resources that can be used to estimate required sample sizes and power. Given the widespread availability of these resources, it is rare that a researcher will need to manually calculate statistical power. All the researcher needs to know is three of the four factors influencing power and the tables or software will determine the value of the fourth factor. The only challenge is determining the value of the three factors. The researcher is typically estimating either the minimum sample size possible or maximum power possible. When estimating the minimum sample size possible, power is typically set at a value between 0.80 and 0.99. When estimating the maximum power, the sample size is set to a value that is determined by practical considerations (e.g. time, available resources and size of the population of interest). The convention is to set α equal to 0.05 or 0.01 (Cohen, 1994). Effect sizes tend to be the most challenging variable to determine, as various types of quantitative analysis are associated with different types of effect size indicators and the researcher may need to rely on a fair amount of subjective judgement.

Box 3.4   Estimating statistical power

Brian needs to conduct a study of the relationship between awareness of in-store advertising of a carbonated beverage and consumer purchase intentions of that carbonated beverage. The company making the carbonated beverage will offer a coupon for a free beverage to every consumer who completes the survey about their purchase intentions and awareness of the in-store advertising. The company has told Brian that they will give him 50 coupons for the study. Before he starts the study, Brian wants to conduct a power analysis to determine how likely he is to find a relationship if one exists. To conduct his power analysis, he sets α equal to 0.05, the sample size to 50, the effect size to 0.20 for a small effect size (see Cohen, 1992) and determines that a correlation will be the analysis (see Part III of Chapter 4). To conduct the power analysis, Brian uses G*Power (Faul et al., 2007) which is a freely available power analysis software program that can be downloaded from the internet. Inputting these values into the program, he estimates that his power will only be 0.40 with a sample of 50. He then uses the software to determine how large the sample needs to be for a power of 0.80. The analysis indicates that he will need 153 participants. Brian tells the company that he will need 103 additional coupons in order to ensure that the research has a reasonable chance of success in determining whether the in-store advertisements are in fact related to purchase intentions.

Effect sizes can be determined using a number of different strategies. First, the simplest strategy is to use rules of thumb about the values for small, medium and large effect sizes (see Cohen, 1988, 1992). Second, one can estimate the smallest value of the effect that would be of interest. When the research involves substantial resources and carries more than a minimal amount of risk to the participants, this strategy may help the researcher determine whether conducting the study is a prudent idea. If the sample sizes required to achieve adequate power, based on the smallest effect size that would be of interest, are far greater than what is possible, the execution of the research may not be justified. Third, one can review the literature for the size of the effects that have been found in previous similar research. Particularly useful are the results of studies that report meta-analytic effect sizes. If the specific effect size needed is not reported in a meta-analysis, it may be possible to transform statistics that are commonly reported (e.g. means and standard deviations, correlations) into the desired effect size (see Rosenthal, 1991). Lastly, one can use empirical strategies, such as pilot studies or Monte Carlo studies (i.e. computer simulations). When possible, we strongly recommend the use of effect size estimates from meta-analyses and empirical or simulation studies.

Sampling methods

Just as critical as obtaining a sample of sufficient size is the process by which the sample is identified and selected. As was described in Chapter 1, the need to draw inferences about a population from a sample was the driving force behind the development of many early quantitative analyses. It was also a driving force in the development of probability and non-probability based strategies for selecting samples that will be representative of the population of interest and increase the likelihood that results obtained from one sample can be replicated in other samples from the same population. From a quantitative analysis perspective, this is important for two reasons. First, representativeness can lead to sample statistics that are unbiased estimates of population parameters. Second, representativeness can produce these unbiased estimates in the most efficient way (i.e. with the smallest sample possible). Both of these points ultimately relate to the generalizability of the sample statistics as estimates of the population parameters.

There are some cases where it is feasible and desirable to collect data from every member of a population. In these cases, sampling is not needed and a census is collected. But in most situations, a sample must be drawn from the population. The process of selecting a sample starts by defining the population of interest for the specific research question. The population can be large (e.g. all males and females) or small (e.g. European biotechnology start-up companies at the initial funding stage). The only requirement is that it can be clearly defined. Although the number of elements (i.e. people, events, objects) in a population does not impact on its definition, the size will have an impact on the sampling method chosen, as we describe later in this chapter. Once the population is defined, a sampling frame is constructed for the probability methods and sampling is initiated for non-probability methods. The sampling frame is a list of individual elements in the population. Elements are the people, objects, events or pieces of information that will be sampled. For example, in a study on the relationship between stock price and corporate governance practices in publicly traded Asian companies, a researcher may use the directory of companies listed on the Hong Kong Stock Exchange as the sampling frame.

All sampling frames will have some members of the population that are missing. Thus, there is a difference between the population and the sample frame. This difference contributes to the difference in the values of sample statistics and population parameters. The difference between population parameters and sample statistics is referred to as sampling error. The sources of sampling error can be random or systematic factors. An example of a random source of sampling error would be that some companies listed on the Hong Kong Stock Exchange were mistakenly left off the list of companies traded at the exchange. The key to random sampling error is that an element of a population being excluded from the sampling frame was simply chance. Systematic sources of sampling error, on the other hand, occur because there are systematic factors influencing whether an element of a population is included in the sampling frame.

Systematic sources of sampling error can take a number of forms. They can occur because there is a known or unknown systematic factor related to an element of a population being excluded from the sampling frame. For example, companies listed on the Hong Kong Stock Exchange for less than one year are not included on the list of the population and are eventually excluded from the sampling frame. In this case, time is a systematic factor related to the likelihood of being included in the sampling frame. Systematic sources of sampling error can also occur because the sampling frame is poorly defined and constructed. In this example, the population of interest is publicly traded Asian companies, but the sampling frame is defined and constructed using only the Hong Kong Stock Exchange. This sampling frame excludes all Asian companies listed on other Asian and global stock exchanges. The goal at each stage of any sampling method is to minimize the sampling error in general and avoid systematic sources of sampling error.

There are a number of different methods that can be used to select the sample. These methods can be grouped into two categories: probability and non-probability sampling methods. In probability sampling methods, each element of the sampling frame has a non-zero probability of being selected into the sample and the probability is known. For example, in the simplest case scenario, each element of a 1000 element sampling frame has a 0.001 probability of being selected into the sample. Probability sampling methods include simple random sampling, stratified sampling, systematic sampling and cluster sampling. For non-probability sampling, the probability of any element being selected into the sample is unknown. Non-probability sampling methods include quota sampling, purposive sampling, snowball sampling and convenience sampling.

Although these methods are typically considered in terms of sampling people in the context of survey methods, they can also be applied to sampling events or objects and other research methods. For example, the sampling methods discussed in this chapter are often used in operational quality control programs to identify samples of products for quality testing. Likewise, researchers studying organizational culture may use these methods to sample organizational and employee communications for text and content analysis. They are also often used to select specific events for analysis such as sampling accidents in the transportation industry or sampling days from which to collect stock market performance. Thus, these methods have applicability to any situation where a researcher needs to obtain a sample for quantitative analyses.

Probability sampling methods

The defining characteristics of probability sampling methods are that the probability of each element in the sampling frame being selected into the sample is known and it is not zero. Probability sampling methods possess a number of advantages over non-probability methods. A main advantage is that they tend to produce sample statistics that are more accurate estimates of population parameters than would be achieved through non-probability methods. Probability methods can also achieve these more accurate estimates with a smaller sample size than would be required by non-probability methods. Probability sampling methods differ in their level of analysis and in the degree to which they divide the sampling frame into more homogenous groups based on the characteristics of the sample.

Simple random sampling

In simple random sampling, each element of the sampling frame has an equal probability of being selected into the sample. The process of selecting elements from the sampling frame is completely random. The random selection can be done using computer software to randomly select a certain number or percentage elements from a sample frame. The researcher can randomly sample elements from a sampling frame with or without replacing the element in the sampling frame. If an element is replaced, the element has the opportunity to be sampled again. Although both methods are viable, sampling without replacement is more common. Many quantitative analyses require elements within the sample to be independent of one another and each element is represented in the data only once, which is consistent with sampling without replacement.

Stratified sampling

One limitation of simple random sampling is that because it is completely random, the final sample may not include elements with characteristics that it is important to have represented. That is, there may be insufficient representation of certain groups in the sample and too much homogeneity in the sample overall. When this is the case, stratified random sampling is a better method as it can ensure that the final sample contains elements with the desired characteristics. In stratified sampling, the sampling frame is divided into groups based on characteristics of the elements. The

groups are called strata and the elements within the strata are similar in characteristics. Common characteristics used to create strata include industry, age, gender,
county and postal code. Any available characteristics could be used. However, it is
recommended only using strata that represent critical characteristics that are essential to have represented in the sample (e.g. stratifying on industry to ensure every
industry is represented). This method provides the benefit of homogeneity between
elements within the strata which is useful for quantitative analyses examining difference between strata. Once the strata are created, random samples can be taken from
within each stratum. The size of the samples randomly drawn from each stratum can
be proportionate to the size of the stratum in the population or can be disproportionate. If some of the strata are small and the interest is in elements within each stratum,
then disproportionate sampling may be the better choice as it will ensure sufficient
sample sizes in each stratum. However, if the interest is in estimating a parameter for
the population, then proportionate sampling is the better choice.

Systematic sampling

In systematic sampling, the selection of elements from the sampling frame is not
completely at random. Instead, the sampling frame is ordered in some fashion and
then elements are selected in a repeating pattern of a fixed interval. For example,
a researcher interested in risk-taking behaviour among stock traders could use an
alphabetized list of names of traders in a financial services company and sample
every fifth trader on the list until the desired number of traders has been obtained.
The researcher could start at the first name on the list or randomly select a starting point. Like all probability sampling methods, the probability of an element being
selected is known. This method will essentially produce a random sample unless there
is some systematic factor embedded in the ordering of the list that corresponds to
the sampling interval.

Cluster sampling

In some instances, it may not be feasible to sample at the level of the individual
element in the sampling frame. Instead, a higher level grouping, called a cluster,
may be used with data collected from all of the individual elements in the selected
clusters. Depending on the variable used to sample the clusters, the resulting sample within each cluster may be highly heterogeneous or, conversely, highly homo-
geneous. The major disadvantage is that cluster sampling is less efficient than
simple random sampling or stratified sampling. Therefore, larger sample sizes will
be needed when using cluster sampling. However, cluster sampling may be more
practical and less costly in many instances.

Box 3.5   Cluster sampling

Karen is a researcher interested in the relationships between stress, mode of commuting to work and commute time. Instead of randomly sampling individuals living in major Asian cities, she randomly samples postal codes of neighbourhoods within a 150 km distance of a major Asian city. She then sends a questionnaire to every household in these postal codes. In this case, she is using cluster sampling as a higher level group variable (i.e. postal codes) to select the sample.

A variation of cluster sampling is multi-stage sampling. In this variant, clusters are randomly sampled at the first stage and then elements within the cluster (e.g. narrower clusters or individual elements) are randomly sampled in the following stages. For example, a researcher interested in corporate ethics policies might randomly select industries and then randomly select companies in those industries. Alternatively, a researcher may be interested in employee recognition practices in manufacturing organizations. The researcher could randomly select manufacturing organizations, then randomly select supervisors and then randomly select employees working for these supervisors. As these examples demonstrate, there can be two stages in the sampling, or the sampling could involve many stages.

Non-probability sampling methods

The defining characteristic of non-probability sampling methods is that the probability of an element being selected is unknown. The primary advantages of non-probability methods are ease of use, control over whether elements with very specific characteristics are included in the sample, and not requiring a predefined sampling frame. In fact, there may not be a sampling frame. These benefits are why non-probability sampling methods are commonly used in both academic and applied research. One could argue that many of the new technology-enabled methods of sampling (e.g. crowd sourcing) that have been popularized are non-probability methods.

Purposeful and quota sampling

In purposeful and quota sampling, the sample elements are intentionally selected based on their possession of characteristics relevant to the research question. With purposeful sampling, an individual who is deemed an expert identifies specific sample elements or clusters that will be representative of the population. For example, in a research study on effective accounting practices, a government regulator may identify companies that are seen as having highly effective accounting practices. This

method has the potential, especially in populations of a limited size, t
representative samples. However, the quality of this method deper
quality of the expert and their judgements.

With quota sampling, a fixed number of sample elements with par
istics (e.g. female, under 30 years of age) are sampled. The sampli
the desired number has been reached. The quotas can be determined by the re-
sentation of the particular characteristics in the population of interest (e.g. general
population, customer base).

Box 3.6   Quota sampling

Supershoes of Russia is a retailer interested in gathering customer opinions on its
ideas for a new athletic shoe. It knows that its customers can be divided into 30%
male over 30 years of age, 40% female over 30 years of age, 20% female under
30 years of age and 10% male under 30 years of age. To ensure that they select a
sample of 1000 customers that is representative of these gender and age groups,
they send 300 surveys to males over 30 years of age, 400 surveys to females over
30 years of age, 200 surveys to females under 30 years of age and 100 surveys to
males under 30 years of age.

Snowball sampling

Snowball sampling is not one specific method per se, but a process by which additional elements can be sampled once the initial sample has been contacted. In
snowball sampling, a researcher creates an initial sample using any of the methods
discussed in this chapter. The researcher asks participants in the sample to complete
the research and then send an invitation to participate in the study to others that
are in their social and professional networks. If a researcher lacks a sampling frame
or has a limited capacity to contact research participants, this method can be useful.
For example, snowball sampling can be particularly useful with hard-to-reach groups
(e.g. executives, the chronically unemployed). Individuals in these groups are much
more likely to respond to an invitation to participate in research when it comes from
someone they know than when it comes from an unknown researcher or organization.

Convenience sampling

A convenience sample is constructed from whoever may be readily available. This
is often referred to as haphazard sampling (Saunders, 2012). In academic research,
convenience samples are synonymous with participant or subject pools of university
students. In applied research, convenience samples come in a number of forms. They

include using employees who happen to be in the cafeteria at a particular time of the day, customers who volunteer to participate in surveys and market research, individuals who are exiting a particular train station at a particular time of the day or individuals who happen to be walking down the street where the researcher is soliciting participants. The primary characteristic, regardless of the type of research, is that the sample is constructed using sample elements that are readily available in a given context.

Convenience samples are often disparaged and justifiably so in many cases. Certainly, convenience samples cannot be recommended when the interest is generalizing from a sample to a population on research questions about opinions, behaviours or attitudes. The results are likely to be biased and unrepresentative of the population. However, they may be appropriate for research questions examining basic fundamental processes that are not likely to vary in their form or function between people. For example, research in the organizational neurosciences often uses convenience samples of university students. When studying the neural basis of affective reactions to negative feedback, convenience sampling is likely to produce representative results. When used appropriately, convenience sampling can be a useful sampling method. When used inappropriately, the results derived from the sample have little value. As a general rule, convenience samples should not be the default choice of sampling method and careful thought should be given to the implications of using this method.

Part II summary

Researchers must make choices about the basic components of the size of sample needed for a research study and how that sample will be selected. Both choices have implications for the quantitative analyses that will be conducted once the data are collected as they impact on the statistical power of the quantitative analyses, on the representativeness of the results for the intended population and on the generalizability of the results. Researchers can determine the sample size by conducting a power analysis. The power analysis requires the researcher to specify a desired level of power, expected effect size and *Type I error* rate. The analysis will indicate the sample size that is needed to achieve the desired level of power given the effect size and *Type I error* rate.

In addition to sample size choices, researchers must select a method to identify that sample. There are a number of probability (e.g. random, stratified, systematic and cluster) and non-probability (e.g. purposive, quota, snowball and convenience) sampling methods available to researchers to select their samples. With probability methods, the probability of selecting an element into the sample is known and it is not zero. With non-probability methods, the probability of selecting an element into the sample is unknown. As we noted in this chapter, there is no sampling method that is always preferable to the others. As with all choices involving research design and quantitative analysis, the best method will depend on the nature of the research question and the desired conclusions.

4

CONDUCTING QUANTITATIVE DATA ANALYSIS

This chapter describes the process of selecting and conducting quantitative analyses. This process starts with a number of steps that a researcher must take to understand the properties of the data collected and to prepare the data for the subsequent quantitative analyses. The results of these steps can determine the types of conclusions that can be drawn from the subsequent hypothesis tests using quantitative analyses. Furthermore, these analyses can determine whether the planned quantitative analyses will be appropriate.

After the data have been prepared for analysis in accordance with the guidelines in Part I of this chapter, the actual process of analysing the data to test the hypotheses can begin. This process begins with choosing appropriate quantitative analyses. There are many types of inferential quantitative analyses and the decision for which analysis to use depends on the nature of the hypothesis as well as the scales of numerical measurement. The decision tree presented in Figure 4.1 provides an overview of the quantitative analyses covered in this chapter and insights into how to choose the appropriate analysis. The first point of consideration is often the design of the study, as discussed in Chapter 3. It is important to note that many quantitative analyses can be used with many study designs. The information presented in the decision tree is a simplification of the process based on the most common analyses used for certain designs. A second consideration is the number of variables involved in the hypothesis. A third consideration is the scale of numerical measurement of the variables (i.e. nominal, ordinal, interval and ratio). This point is crucial, as it dictates whether it is appropriate to use parametric or non-parametric quantitative analyses.

Parametric analyses assume that the underlying population takes the form of a particular distribution that has known characteristics. These assumptions can be met when

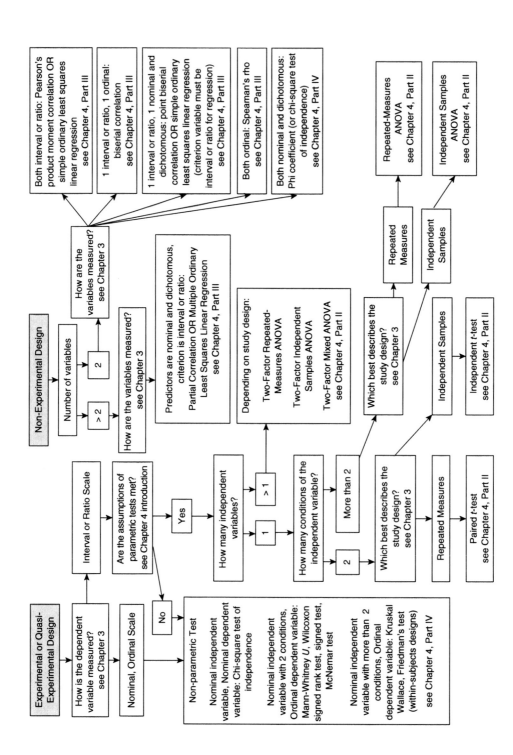

Figure 4.1 Decision tree for selecting the appropriate quantitative analysis

the dependent variable is measured using interval or ratio scales. Non-parametric tests (sometimes called distribution-free tests) do not require the same assumptions about a population distribution. When the dependent variable is ordinal or nominal data, assumptions about the distribution cannot be made, so non-parametric tests must be used (see Part IV of this chapter). For most study designs, there are parametric and non-parametric alternatives to test hypotheses.

There are advantages and drawbacks to using both parametric and non-parametric tests. The drawback to using non-parametric tests is that they are less statistically powerful than parametric tests. Because they cannot rely on assumptions about a distribution to compute probabilities, non-parametric tests must rely on more conservative approaches to estimate probability. On the other hand, a drawback of parametric tests is that they require that a set of assumptions be met. The assumptions include that the sample data come from a population that resembles a normal distribution and that the variances of the populations being compared are equal (this concept is called homogeneity of variance). These assumptions need not be met when using non-parametric tests.

In the following sections of this chapter, we describe the various types of quantitative analyses that are most commonly used to test hypotheses, beginning with those that are commonly used with experimental and quasi-experimental designs, and then those commonly used with non-experimental designs. This is followed by a discussion of non-parametric quantitative analyses.

PART I: DATA PREPARATION AND DESCRIPTIVE QUANTITATIVE ANALYSES

In this section, we outline the specific steps that a researcher should take before engaging in quantitative analyses. These steps are summarized in Table 4.1. The steps will help the researcher understand the properties of the data collected and to prepare the data for the subsequent quantitative analyses. We cannot overemphasize the importance of thoughtfully and thoroughly executing these steps. The

Table 4.1   Steps in data preparation and descriptive quantitative analysis

Step	Activity
1	Data importation and initial evaluation of the accuracy of the data
2	Screening for missing data
3	Executing data transformations
4	Examining the distribution of the data and evaluating outliers
5	Evaluating the relationships between items and composite scales

quantitative analysis chosen and the nature of the conclusions drawn from the analyses will depend on the information provided by these steps.

Although this process is presented as a series of linear steps, the process may be quite circular. For example, an examination of the distribution of the data in step 4 may necessitate a return to step 3 to transform the data to ensure it meets the assumptions of the planned quantitative analyses.

Step 1: Data importation and initial evaluation of the accuracy of the data

First, the data should be imported or entered into a statistical analysis software package (e.g. IBM's SPSS, R, SAS or Excel). Most statistical analysis software packages offer a variety of options for importing data in a variety of formats (e.g. text files, spreadsheets). For most of the analyses reviewed here, the data are structured such that each row is a case (e.g. person, event or object) and each column is a variable. Although it is not required, it is best practice to ensure that each case has a unique identifier (e.g. random id number, customer id number, employee id number, etc.). An example of a typical data file from Microsoft Excel is presented in Figure 4.2. In the figure, each row represents an individual who responded to a customer survey. The columns represent the variables in this data set. The first column contains the respondents' unique ID number and the remaining columns represent the responses to each question on the survey.

Once the data have been imported or entered, the data should be screened for data entry errors, impossible data values and other aberrant data values. The screening should be performed for every variable in the data set. The screening can be performed using a frequency analysis. A frequency analysis provides information about the number of observations at each observed value of a variable, as well as

	A id	B q1	C q2	D q3	E q4	F q5	G q6	H q7	I q8
1	id	q1	q2	q3	q4	q5	q6	q7	q8
2	1	0	1	4	4	4	4	4	4
3	2	0	0	5	4	4	4	5	5
4	3	0	0	4	4	4	4		4
5	4	0	0	3	4	4	3	3	4
6	5	0	0	5	4	5	5	5	5
7	6	1	0	4		4	4	4	4
8	7	0	1	4	3	4	5	4	4
9	8	1	1	4	4	4	3	3	3
10	9	1	0	5	2	4	4	5	5
11	10	0	1	4	4	4	3	4	
12	11	1	1	5	4	4	3	4	3
13	12	0		4	3	4	4	4	3
14	13	0	0	4	3	4	4	4	4
15	14	0	1		3	4	4	4	3

Figure 4.2 Example data file structure in Microsoft Excel

the frequency of missing data. In addition to providing information about the number of observations at each value of a variable and the percentage of observations at each possible value, frequency analyses commonly provide the cumulative number of observations and the cumulative percentage. A frequency analysis can be performed in Excel using the 'countif' function for the simple frequency and the 'frequency' function for cumulative frequencies. The percentages can be computed by dividing the frequency for a specific value by the total number of observations. A frequency analysis can serve many purposes and will be used in several of the steps described in this section. An example frequency analysis is presented in Table 4.2.

Table 4.2   Example frequency table of response data

	Frequency	Cumulative Frequency	Percentage	Cumulative Percentage
Strongly disagree (1)	34	34	1.7%	1.7%
Disagree (2)	132	166	6.4%	8.1%
Neutral (3)	291	457	14.2%	22.3%
Agree (4)	487	944	23.7%	46.0%
Strongly agree (5)	1051	1995	51.2%	97.2%
9	7	2002	0.3%	97.6%
Missing	50	2052	2.4%	100.0%
Total	**2052**	**2052**	**100.00%**	**100.00%**

In this table, one can determine which values appear in the data set, how many times the values occur, whether those values represent possible values that the data could take and how much data is missing. For example, if a five-point (1–5) rating scale were used, values above five and below one are not possible in this scoring scheme. Using the data in Table 4.2, the value of 9 is not possible if a 1–5 scoring scheme was used in the research. Before concluding that a datum point represents an impossible value, the researcher should verify the data coding scheme to ensure that the value is not possible. The search for impossible or unlikely values applies to non-rating scale data as well. For example, ages of 180 and salaries of $400 million Euros are unlikely, if not impossible, and should be verified.

Box 4.1   Computing frequencies

Alistair is a career development specialist who has been asked to examine the career trajectories of his company's current managerial workforce. He starts by examining the number of promotions that the managers have received in the last

(Continued)

(Continued)

eight years. He finds that the maximum number of promotions is four and the minimum is one. He computes the frequency of one, two, three and four promotions. In Excel, he uses the 'countif' function to compute the frequency of one promotion: =countif(number of promotions variable, 1). He repeats the process for the remaining number of promotions. Alistair then computes the cumulative frequency starting with one promotion. In Excel, he uses the 'frequency' function to compute the cumulative frequency of one promotion: =frequency(number of promotions variable, 1). These formulas are presented next to the results to illustrate their use. He repeats the process for the remaining number of promotions. Alistair finds that most managers have had three or four promotions over the past eight years and appear to be making a good degree of career progress.

	A	B	C	D	E
1	Number of Promotions		Number of Promotions	Frequency	
2	1		1	6	=COUNTIF(A2:A19, C2)
3	4		2	3	=COUNTIF(A2:A19, C3)
4	1		3	4	=COUNTIF(A2:A19, C4)
5	4		4	5	=COUNTIF(A2:A19, C5)
6	3				
7	4				
8	1				
9	4		Number of Promotions	Cummulative frequency	
10	3		1	6	=FREQUENCY(A2:A19, C10)
11	2		2	9	=FREQUENCY(A2:A19, C11)
12	1		3	13	=FREQUENCY(A2:A19, C12)
13	1		4	18	=FREQUENCY(A2:A19, C13)
14	1				
15	2				
16	3				
17	4				
18	3				
19	2				

If a researcher discovers that there are impossible or highly unlikely values in the data, there are several actions that can be taken. The researcher can check the data against the original data file or data collection materials, such as completed questionnaires, to verify the accuracy of the data. Any necessary corrections to the data can be made. If the impossible value in the data is correct, the researcher will need to delete the specific datum point or remove all of the data from the specific case. Although both are viable options, we recommend that the individual datum point be deleted and treated as missing data. However, if a particular case has several instances of impossible or unlikely data, the entire case should be removed.

Alternatively, the researcher can simply delete any problematic data or cases without any review of the original data. This may be the option of choice when the data set is very large and the number of problematic datum points is very small. If the data were manually entered, a random sample of the entries should be selected and audited to ensure accuracy of the data even if no problematic datum points were identified. Regardless of the strategy to address problematic data, the researcher should conduct a frequency analysis after the review and modifications to verify that the problems are resolved.

Step 2: Screening for missing data

Part of the data screening process includes an evaluation of the amount of missing data and the reasons for it (Graham, 2009; Little and Rubin, 2002). The presence of missing data can lead to results that may not be representative of the intended population, lead to threats to the internal validity of the research or lead to insufficient data for tests of hypotheses (i.e. low statistical power). A primary consideration with missing data is whether it is missing at random or missing systematically. Missing data at random is the case when the probability of missing data is unrelated to any other variable and to the value of the variable with the missing data. In other words, the missing data are not related to the response that would have been provided or to any other variable and characteristic. For example, missing data for entrepreneurs on questions about revenue would need to be unrelated to the level of revenue or to other characteristics of the respondent (e.g. type of business) to be considered missing at random. Data that are missing at random does not necessarily create a situation where the results will not be representative of the intended population. Data that are missing following a more systematic pattern (e.g. missing data only on the sensitive survey items, no revenue reported only by failing business owners or missing data only for certain types of events or people) can create results that are not representative of the population from which the sample was drawn. This type of missing data is often referred to as non-ignorable (Little and Rubin, 2002). In contrast, data that are missing at random may be ignorable.

Missing data could arise for a number of reasons including intentional or unintentional non-response, the respondent ran out of time, the respondent stopped the data collection process before completion, the data collection tool experienced an error while capturing data (e.g. a server experiencing a loss of internet connectivity) or data entry error(s) from importing the data. It is important to evaluate the reasons for missing data as they have potential implications for the tests of the hypotheses. Missing data caused by data entry or data importation error can easily be fixed if the original data files or materials are available. Data that are missing because of non-response, careless responding or dropout are more difficult to address as they are likely to be missing systematically and are non-ignorable.

The level of missing data that can be tolerated will depend on the size of the sample, the research design and whether the data are missing at random or missing systematically. Missing data are a much larger concern when sample sizes are small and in longitudinal research (i.e. data collected at multiple points in time). When the data are missing at random, the level of missing data that could be tolerated may be greater than when data are missing systematically. When the data are missing systematically, complex modelling is needed that includes factors to capture the missing data (see Little and Rubin, 2002 for a review of these methods). If it is missing at random, there are a number of options available to the researcher, including deleting the case or using imputation methods to replace the missing data (see Alison, 2001; Graham, 2009; or Little and Rubin, 2002 for a review of these methods). A frequency analysis can be used to examine the amount of missing data that is present. For example, in the data presented in Table 4.2 there are 50 respondents with missing values. This represents a very small percentage of the total sample.

Step 3: Executing data transformations

Often, management and business research includes measures that are scored in different directions. On an inventory of personality, for example, responses at the higher end of the response scale may indicate high levels of the personality trait on some items, but it may indicate low levels of the trait on different items (i.e. reverse scoring or keying). If reverse scoring is used, the data may need to be recoded such that the responses are in the same direction. For example, there are two items on the Shockley and Allen (2010) need for affiliation measure that are reverse coded (see Table 3.1). Typically, this type of transformation is easily performed in most statistical software packages using data recoding routines. Likewise, data exported from organizational databases often come in the form of text instead of numbers (e.g. 'female' instead of 1). These data need to be recoded into numerical data in order to perform quantitative analyses. Some statistical software programs have automatic recoding procedures that are highly useful with text data.

Box 4.2   Recoding data

Manufacturing Vendors International is an industry association that commissioned a survey to understand the manufacturing strategies that its members are using. Questions were answered using a five-point rating scale. Most of the questions were worded such that higher scores represented more positive opinions about the current strategy. However, one question on the survey was worded, 'Our current manufacturing strategy is incomprehensible'. Higher scores on this item represent negative opinions. This item needed to be recoded so that a score of 1 becomes a 5, a score of 2 becomes a 4, a score of 4 becomes a 2 and a score of 5 becomes a 1.

As was introduced in Chapter 3, many management and business measures utilize multiple items to assess a construct (e.g. personality, socioeconomic status, customer loyalty). These individual items are combined (i.e. aggregated) into what are called composite scores or scale scores. For example, the 10 items on a personality inventory that assess extroversion could be summed or averaged to create an extroversion score for each individual. When creating composite scores based on sums (e.g. test data), the researcher needs to consider the impact of missing data on the composite score. When the data are summed, missing data lowers the possible score that an individual may achieve. In many cases when working with sums, it is advisable to compute a summed composite only when the individual has a certain percentage of complete data (e.g. data available on 80% of the observations or items).

Researchers frequently transform their data from its normal metric into a mathematical metric such as the natural logarithm. The goal of these transformations is to create a desired distribution (e.g. a symmetric bell-shaped distribution) when the distribution of the observed data take an undesirable distribution (e.g. an extreme skew). It is important to remember that transformation can change the data that the researcher is using in the subsequent quantitative analyses, but they do not change the fact that the data do not naturally take the transformed shape, and any interpretations need to be made in reference to the transformed data, not the original metric of the data.

One of the most common transformations is the z-score or standardized score. Z-scores are computed as follows:

$$Z = \frac{X - M}{\sigma}$$ Eq. 4.1

where M is the mean of the sample, X is the value of a particular datum point and σ is the standard deviation of the sample. To compute the z-score, one first computes the mean and standard deviation (see the next section). Next, one subtracts the mean from each score. Finally, one divides the difference between the score and the mean by the standard deviation. Z-scores can be interpreted as standard deviations. The number for the z-score represents the number of standard deviations the datum point is from the mean.

Box 4.3   Computing z-scores

Taleb is a quality control specialist for a computer chip manufacturer. He has been asked to examine the rate of defective computer chips for the past year and compute the standardized score for each month. Using Excel, Taleb first computes the mean and standard deviation for the rate of defective chips for the entire year. Next, he computes the standardized scores for January using the standardize function in

(Continued)

(Continued)

Excel: =standardize(January, rate of defective chips, mean, standard deviation). He repeats this process for the remaining months. He finds that in the month of July the defect rate was 2.08 standard deviations above the mean.

	A	B	C	D
	Month	Rate of Defective Chips	z-score	
1				
2	January	0.84%	-0.66	=STANDARDIZE(B2,B14,B15)
3	February	1.23%	-0.44	=STANDARDIZE(B3,B14,B15)
4	March	0.98%	-0.58	=STANDARDIZE(B4,B14,B15)
5	April	1.18%	-0.47	=STANDARDIZE(B5,B14,B15)
6	May	1.07%	-0.53	=STANDARDIZE(B6,B14,B15)
7	June	4.31%	1.28	=STANDARDIZE(B7,B14,B15)
8	July	5.76%	2.08	=STANDARDIZE(B8,B14,B15)
9	August	4.76%	1.53	=STANDARDIZE(B9,B14,B15)
10	September	0.95%	-0.6	=STANDARDIZE(B10,B14,B15)
11	October	1.13%	-0.5	=STANDARDIZE(B11,B14,B15)
12	November	0.88%	-0.64	=STANDARDIZE(B12,B14,B15)
13	December	1.20%	-0.46	=STANDARDIZE(B13,B14,B15)
14	Mean	2.02%		=AVERAGE(B2:B13)
15	Standard Deviation	0.0179		=STDEV.S(B2:B13)

Step 4: Examining the distribution of the data and evaluating outliers

Once the initial data screening has been performed, the shape of the distribution of the data should be examined. Many of the quantitative analyses used to test hypotheses make assumptions about the shape of the distribution that need to be considered. There are a number of statistics and graphics that that can be used to evaluate the shape of a distribution of data. Graphical methods present tables or graphs that visually represent the entire distribution of data. The statistical methods produce a small set of numbers that can be used to describe the shape of the distribution. We first consider the graphical methods that can be used and then the statistical methods. We strongly recommend that researchers evaluate the shape of a distribution of data using multiple methods.

In addition to considering the shape of the distribution and the degree to which the assumptions of the planned quantitative analyses are met, the researcher should also evaluate the presence of extreme data (i.e. outliers). Outliers can substantially impact on the results of quantitative analyses by masking results or spuriously creating them. Each of the methods reviewed offers specific techniques and rules to identify outliers. In cases where outliers are found, the researcher should flag them in the data. For example, the researcher could create a new variable in the data set that has the value of '1' for the cases that have outliers on any of the variables and use '0' for every other case. When running the quantitative analyses, the researcher can use this new variable to include or exclude the outliers to determine their impact on the results of the analyses.

Graphical methods

A reasonable first step is to examine the frequency distribution of the data (from step 1). This will provide a first indication of the shape of the distribution and any potential outliers. The distribution can be displayed using frequency tables or a histogram and bar chart. As previously noted, the frequency table displays each value that appears in the data and the number of times the value appears (see Table 4.2). In addition to the simple count for each value, the cumulative count (i.e. cumulative frequency), the percentage of the sample at each possible value and the cumulative percentage are displayed. In Table 4.2, one can see that few values appear at the lower end of the response scale and that the majority of the response data are at the upper end of the scale. In fact, 51.2% of the data occurs at response option 5.

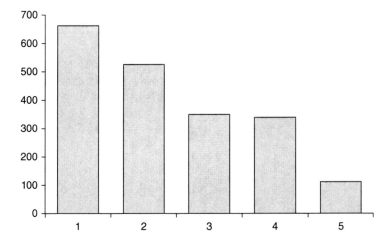

Figure 4.3 Example of a positively skewed distribution

Histograms and bar charts are a graphical representation of the frequency table (see Figure 4.3). In a histogram or bar chart, the x-axis contains the possible values on the specific variable. The y-axis contains the frequency. The difference between the two is that histograms are used for continuous data and the bars in the graph touch. Bar charts, where the bars do not touch, are used when the data are not truly continuous. These graphs can be created in most statistical software. In Excel, they can be created using the chart wizard. As can be seen in Figure 4.3, the data are concentrated at the lower end of the scale with a tail that points toward the more positive numbers. This pattern is called a positively skewed distribution. A negatively skewed distribution shows the opposite pattern, with the tail of the distribution pointing toward the lower end of the scale, as is shown in Figure 4.4.

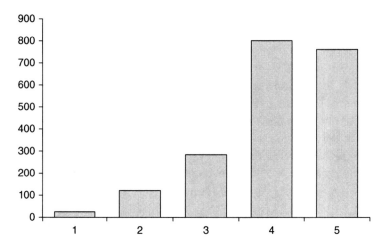

Figure 4.4   Example of a negatively skewed distribution

The distribution of the data can also take a more symmetrical shape. Simply put, in a symmetrical distribution, the right and left sides of the distribution are mirror images. The normal distribution is the classic example of a symmetrical distribution. Another notable example is the uniform distribution in which all of the values have the same frequency and the distribution takes the shape of a rectangle. An example of a symmetric distribution is presented in Figure 4.5.

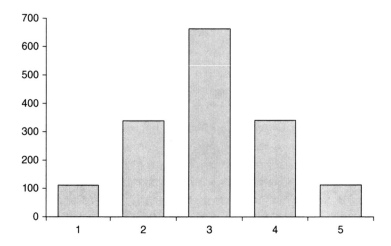

Figure 4.5   Example of a unimodal symmetric distribution

Bar charts and histograms can be useful as an initial evaluation for the possibility of outliers. If there are one or more datum points that are clearly removed from the rest of the distribution, it is an indication of potential outliers. This visual inspection is not a definitive test of outliers. Rather, it is an initial indicator that additional inspection is needed.

There are a variety of additional graphical procedures under the label of exploratory data analysis (Tukey, 1977) that can be utilized to describe a distribution. A stem-and-leaf plot is presented in Figure 4.6. This graph is similar to a histogram in that the length of the bars represents the frequency. The graph is presented vertically and is constructed using the actual values in the data. The value (e.g. 7) is used as the stem in the graph and the last digit (e.g. 1) is used to create the leaves. The number of times that the last digit is repeated in the leaf represents the frequency of that value. A useful feature of these graphs is that they identify extreme positive or negative values that may be considered outliers.

A boxplot is another graphic that can be used to display the shape of the distribution (see Figure 4.7). These graphs are also often referred to as box and whisker plots. A boxplot essentially creates a box representing the middle 50% of the data.

Frequency	Stem and Leaf
2.00	Extremes (=<50)
1.00	5 . &
1.00	6 . &
14.00	7 . 1579&
39.00	8 . 00123445667899
57.00	9 . 001122233455566788899
96.00	10 . 000111222233444455556667777889999
121.00	11 . 00001112223333444444555566666677778888999
164.00	12 . 00011111222222333333344445555556666777778888889999
179.00	13 . 001111122233333333444444455555566667777888888999999
190.00	14 . 000000011111122222333333344444455555556666666677777788999999
192.00	15 . 000000011122222222333334444444555666666777777788999999999
197.00	16 . 000002222222333333344445555555555666778888889999999
185.00	17 . 001111111123333344444555555555666677777888889999999
164.00	18 . 000000011111223333334444455556666667777777888899
104.00	19 . 0001112222333444444555566667778889999
72.00	20 . 0001222333445556667778889 99
54.00	21 . 0001233444455678899
16.00	22 . 01458&
11.00	23 . 039&
3.00	24 . &
8.00	Extremes (>=246)

Notes:
Stem width: 10.00
Each leaf: 3 case(s)

Figure 4.6 Example of a stem and leaf plot

The box is constructed using the data between the 25th and 75th percentile of the distribution. The distance between the top and bottom of the box is called the interquartile range. The solid line inside the box represents the 50th percentile (i.e. the median). There are several possible methods for determining the length of 'whiskers' in the plot. One can draw the whiskers from the box to: (1) the minimum and maximum values in the data; (2) ± 1.5 times the interquartile range; or (3) an extreme upper and lower percentile (e.g. 5th and 95th percentile).

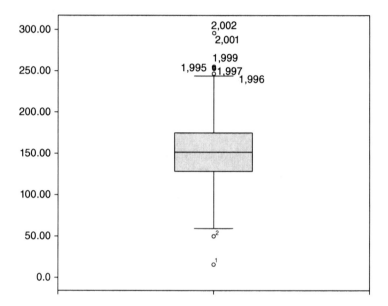

Figure 4.7   Example boxplot

In a boxplot, outliers can be identified as data that are beyond the upper or the lower whisker. As shown in Figure 4.7, these data are represented with a dot on the plot and the case number that the dot represents.

Statistical methods

Descriptive quantitative analyses are used to statistically evaluate the shape of a distribution. Their value is that they can summarize the shape of any distribution, including very large ones, with a limited set of statistics. Descriptive quantitative analyses include measures of central tendency, measures of variability and measures of skew. In general, these descriptive statistics are most appropriately used with data that is on an interval or ratio scale. The examples of the statistical methods presented in this chapter include the Excel formulas adjacent to the results to display the underlying computations.

Measures of central tendency describe the most representative point in a distribution. The mean, median and mode are examples of central tendency measures. The mode is the most commonly occurring value for a variable (i.e. the most frequent value). Any given distribution can have one or many modes. A distribution with one mode is called unimodel. A distribution with two modes is called bimodal. The mode is the only descriptive quantitative analysis appropriately used with nominal data. The median represents the 50th percentile of a variable. That is, the median is the point that divides the distribution into two equal halves. Both the median and the mode are determined from the frequencies of the data. One useful aspect of each is that they are only slightly, or not at all, impacted on by outliers. Therefore, their values can be slightly more stable from sample to sample than the mean.

The mean is the arithmetic average of a set of data. It is computed as the sum of the data for a variable divided by the sample size. It is represented mathematically in Eq. 4.2:

$$M = \frac{\Sigma x}{n}$$
Eq. 4.2

In the equation, Σx is the sum of the values on a variable x, n is the sample size and M is the sample mean (this can also be symbolized as $\bar{x}$). The mean is influenced by outliers. The mean will be pulled in the direction of the most extreme outlier (i.e. increase or decrease in value). If potential outliers are present, the trimmed mean can be used. The trimmed mean drops a certain percentage (e.g. 5%) of the data at the ends of the distribution where the outliers are located.

The relationship between the mean, the median and the mode can be informative about the shape of a distribution. If the three are equal, it indicates a symmetric distribution. In situations where the mean has the smallest value and the mode has the largest value, this indicates a negatively skewed distribution. In the opposite scenario where the mode has the smallest value and the mean the largest, it indicates a positively skewed distribution.

Measures of variability describe the spread of a distribution. The range, variance and standard deviation are examples of variability measures. Measures of variability are most appropriately used with data that is on an interval or ratio scale. The range represents the total variability demarcated by the distance from the largest and smallest value on a variable. In other words, it represents the variability between each of the ends of the distribution. The range is computed as the difference between the maximum and minimum value of a variable. Given this computation, the range is heavily impacted on by the presence of outliers. The range can be useful in the data screening process. For many variables, there is an expected range based on theory or the measurement process. If the values of the range are greater than what would be expected, this may indicate that impossible or inaccurate values exist for the variable. If the values of the range are much smaller than the possible range, it can indicate that there is a restriction in range for the variable. Restriction of range occurs when only a narrow range of the possible values on a variable are represented. For example, there is typically a restriction of range in entrance exam scores for students admitted to top universities such that the scores are high and within a narrow range of the upper end of the possible range.

The variance and standard deviation indicate the variability or spread of the data from the mean. They are most appropriately used with interval or ratio data. The importance of the variance and standard deviation cannot be understated. They play a role in every parametric quantitative analysis covered in this book. The variance represents the average squared deviation from the mean and is mathematically defined in Eq. 4.3:

$$s^2 = \frac{\Sigma(x - M)^2}{n - 1}$$
Eq. 4.3

In the equation, n represents the sample size, x is a datum point on the variable and M is the sample mean. To compute the variance, one takes the difference between each datum point and the mean. Next, one squares those differences and sums them. Finally, one divides the sum by the sample size minus one.

A simple way of conceptualizing the variance is that it represents the average distance between each datum point and the mean in squared units. Given that squared units are not a metric that is typically used, the square root of the variance is taken to produce the standard deviation $(s = \sqrt{s^2})$. The standard deviation represents variability from the mean in the same unit of measurement as the mean. There is no set of guidelines that can be used to determine whether a variance or standard deviation is large or small. Their magnitude can be evaluated only in comparison to the value of the mean. A standard deviation of 100 would seem large if the mean was 150, but very small if the mean was 10,000. The researcher will need to evaluate the variance and standard deviation in comparison to the mean and the expected variability. As discussed in later chapters, for some quantitative analyses, smaller values for the variance and standard deviation are desirable. For other analyses, larger values are more beneficial.

Box 4.4   Computing measures of central tendency and variability

Shreya is an accountant who has been asked to examine the average spending on raw materials and the variability in that spending across her company's nine manufacturing plants in the month of December. Using Excel, Shreya first computes the measures of central tendency. To compute the mode and median, she uses the 'mode' function: =mode(Bristol spending on raw materials :Rio de Janeiro spending on raw materials) and the 'median' function: =median(Bristol spending on raw materials:Rio de Janeiro spending on raw materials). To compute the mean, she uses the 'average' function: =average(Bristol spending on raw materials:Rio de Janeiro spending on raw materials).

Next, Shreya computes the measures of variability. She starts by computing the range. In Excel, she computes the maximum value for the expenses: =max(Bristol spending on raw materials:Rio de Janeiro spending on raw materials) and the minimum value for the expenses: =min(Bristol spending on raw materials:Rio de Janeiro spending on raw materials). The range is computed by subtracting the minimum from the maximum. To compute the variance and standard deviation, she uses the 'var.s' function: =var.s(Bristol spending on raw materials:Rio de Janeiro spending on raw materials) and the 'stdev.s' function: =stdev.s(Bristol spending on raw materials: Rio de Janeiro spending on raw materials).

Shreya finds that on average the plants spent £1,045,666 on raw materials (mean). Half of the plants spent £932,000 or less (median). The most common amount spent was £901,000 (mode). The range in the spending was £499,000. The average difference between the mean and the datum points is £191,354 (standard deviation).

	A	B	C	D	E	F
1	Plant	Expenses for Raw Materials		Mode	£901,000.00	=MODE(B2:B10)
2	Bristol	£1,200,000.00		Median	£932,000.00	=MEDIAN(B2:B10)
3	Shenzhen	£901,000.00		Mean	£1,045,666.67	=AVERAGE(B2:B10)
4	Mexico City	£932,000.00		Maximum	£1,400,000.00	=MAX(B2:B10)
5	Detroit	£1,400,000.00		Minimum	£901,000.00	=MIN(B2:B10)
6	Kiev	£901,000.00		Range	£499,000.00	=E4-E5
7	Johannesburg	£988,000.00		Variance	£36,616,500,000.00	=VAR.S(B2:B10)
8	Manila	£901,000.00		Standard Deviation	£191,354.38	=STDEV.S(B2:B10)
9	Brisbane	£1,267,000.00		Kurtosis	-0.483139893	=KURT(B2:B10)
10	Rio de Janeiro	£921,000.00		Skewness	1.062569029	=SKEW(B2:B10)

The discussion of measures of central tendency and variability has focused on distributions of actual data from a single sample. One can also construct distributions of test statistics. As discussed in detail in Parts II, III and IV of this chapter, each inferential quantitative analysis involves the computation of a value (e.g. t, F, r or b). These values each form a distribution of their own with a set mean and set standard deviation (i.e. a sampling distribution). This concept is of critical importance to null hypothesis significance testing, as these distributions are used to make judgements about probability.

In addition to measures of central tendency and variability, there are a number of statistics that have been designed to quantify the shapes seen in the graphical representations of the distribution. Skewness and kurtosis are examples of these measures. Skewness is a statistic that reflects the degree to which the distribution is symmetric. When a distribution is symmetric, the value of the skewness statistic is 0.00 or very close to 0.00. Larger values indicate a greater degree of skewness (i.e. non-symmetry). It will be negative when the distribution is negatively skewed. A standard error can be computed for the skewness. The standard error is the standard deviation of a sampling distribution. The standard error can be used to determine the number of standard deviations the skewness is from the value of 0.00. If it is more than two standard deviations in either direction, it may indicate a substantial degree of skew in the data. For example, in Box 4.4, the value of the skewness is 1.06 which indicates a highly positively skewed distribution.

Kurtosis reflects the 'peakedness' of a distribution, that is, how pointed or flat a given distribution is relative to a symmetric unimodal distribution. If a distribution is symmetric with a single mode, the value of the kurtosis statistic will be 0.00 or very close to 0.00. Larger values indicate a greater degree of peakedness or flatness to the distribution. Positive values of kurtosis indicate that a distribution is peaked and possesses thick tails (i.e. a *leptokurtic* distribution). Negative values of kurtosis indicate that a distribution is flat and possesses thin tails (i.e. a *platykurtic* distribution). A standard error can be computed for the kurtosis and the standard error can be used to determine the number of standard deviations the kurtosis is from the value of 0.00. If it is more than two standard deviations, it may indicate a substantial degree of departure from a unimodal symmetric distribution. These two measures of the shape of a distribution are not well understood and are often not reported, but they provide useful information about a distribution (DeCarlo, 1997). For example, in Box 4.4, the value of the kurtosis is -0.48 which indicates that the distribution is platykurtic.

Many of the quantitative analyses discussed in Part II and Part III of this chapter require specific assumptions about the shape of the distribution. There are several tests that can be used to determine whether the sample distribution sufficiently takes that shape. To test if the distribution of the data takes a particular distributional shape (e.g. normal), the Kolmogorov-Smirnov test or Shapiro-Wilks test can be used. The Kolmogorov-Smirnov test can determine whether an observed distribution differs from a normal distribution, uniform distribution, exponential distribution or Poisson distribution. This test can be used to determine whether the data conform to a specific theoretical distribution or whether two distributions are different from one another. The Shapiro-Wilks test can be used to determine whether an observed distribution differs from a normal distribution and is particularly useful when sample sizes are small.

Step 5: Evaluating the relationships between items and composite scales

When aggregating variables into composites or scales, a researcher needs to examine the resulting composite or scale in terms of the relationships between the items that constitute the composite or scale. This can be done using measures of relationship such as correlations. Correlations are a family of statistical techniques that assess the direction and strength of the relationship between two or more variables. Correlations are discussed at length in Part III of this chapter. In this context, the researcher should examine the correlations between the variables used to create a composite.

The composite should also be evaluated in terms of its consistency and underlying structure (i.e. dimensionality). Later books in this series will cover these topics in more detail. However, the importance of reliability, or consistency, necessitates a brief discussion of its role as one of the steps taken before performing quantitative analysis. Reliability is a property of the responses to the individual items in a composite. Thus, it is assessed using the responses to each of the items that make up the composite scale, not the composite scores. There are several types of reliability coefficients. First, there are coefficients that evaluate the stability of responses over time. These are often called test-retest or stability coefficients. Correlations between responses at the two different points in time are used to compute this reliability coefficient. Second, there are coefficients that evaluate the equivalence of different items or forms measuring the same construct. These are called equivalence coefficients. Correlations between the different sets of items or forms are used to compute this reliability coefficient.

Lastly, there are coefficients that assess internal consistency. Internal consistency can be thought of as the homogeneity of responses to the items. If the responses to the items are on a continuous scale, Cronbach's alpha can be used. Kuder-Richardson's KR-20 or KR-21 can be used with dichotomous data. These reliability coefficients can range from 0.0 to 1.0 with 1.0 indicating perfect consistency. Although there is no definitive standard for evaluating internal consistency estimates (Pedhazur and Pedhazur-Schmelkin, 1991) and many mistaken beliefs about what constitutes acceptable evidence (Lance et al., 2006), Nunnally's (1978) recommendation that estimates should be .70 for exploratory research and above .90 for practical applications is reasonable. Demonstrating satisfactory reliability estimates is essential. Scales for which the responses demonstrate low levels of reliability are of little value in evaluating research questions.

Part I summary

All quantitative analyses start with a series of steps designed to help the researcher understand the properties of his or her data and prepare the data for the quantitative analyses used to test the research questions and hypotheses of the research study. These steps will help the researcher understand the accuracy, the level of missing data, the central tendency (mean, median and mode) and the variability (range, variance and standard deviation) of a data set. These steps will also help the researcher conduct any necessary transformation to prepare the data for the quantitative analyses. The steps include importing the data and checking their accuracy, screening for missing data, executing data transformations, examining the distribution of the data and evaluating outliers, and evaluating the relationships between items and composite scales (see Table 4.1). The fourth step of this process involves the computation of the mean, median, mode, variance and standard deviation, which are common descriptive quantitative analyses.

The steps outlined in the first part of this chapter will be of use with any data that a researcher may encounter. However, in some situations there are some additional steps that may be necessary. In many cases, the researcher analysing the data is involved in designing and executing the research study and is very familiar with the measures and methods used. However, it is becoming increasingly common that the researcher analysing the data is not involved with the earlier stages of the research (e.g. secondary data). Therefore, the researcher may be less intimately familiar with the nature of the measures collected and elements of the sample or research design that can impact on the quantitative analyses. In these situations, we strongly advocate the researcher ask a number of questions about the data as an additional step that would occur prior to step 1 described in this chapter. These questions include:

1. Who were these data collected from and how were they selected for inclusion in the study?
2. What items were presented to the respondents?
3. What were the possible responses to the items?
4. When were the data collected?
5. What was the context surrounding the data collection?

The response to each of these questions can shape the nature of the performance of the quantitative analyses or affect whether any analyses are performed at all. When the researcher is not involved in the research design and execution, additional caution is needed to ensure that appropriate quantitative analyses are conducted and the results are interpreted correctly.

Box 4.5   Understanding data when the researcher is not involved with data collection

Sun is an analyst for a global financial institution who has been asked by the human resources department to analyse data on the firm's managerial 360-degree feedback program to test research questions about its effectiveness. Sun is not involved with the program and this is the first time she has seen these data. Before analysing the data, Sun asks the following questions:

1. Which employees were these 360 feedback data collected from and how were these employees selected to provide feedback?
2. What items were presented to the employees on the 360 feedback forms?
3. What were the possible responses to the items on the 360 feedback forms?
4. When were the 360 feedback data collected?
5. What was the context surrounding the collection of the 360 feedback data?

She finds that the employees providing feedback were picked by the manager being evaluated, the evaluations of the manager were collected immediately before the employees' salary adjustments were to be determined, the evaluation form contained only items focused on exceptional performance and the manager was present when the employees completed the evaluation forms. Based on this information, Sun concludes that there is little insight that can be gained from analysing the data as it is very unlikely to provide an accurate and representative evaluation of the managers. She does not analyse the data further.

PART II: QUANTITATIVE ANALYSES COMMONLY USED WITH EXPERIMENTAL RESEARCH

This part of the chapter provides guidance on many of the most commonly used quantitative analyses with experimental and quasi-experimental research designs. The presentation of each analysis will cover the basic logic, formula and steps in the computation, and briefly review the major assumptions. We present this information to give a conceptual basis for the formulas; however, in practice, hand calculations are rare. Most quantitative analyses will be conducted using software programs, such as Excel, SPSS, SAS and R. For each quantitative analysis, we describe the process and the functions that can be used to conduct the quantitative analysis using Microsoft Excel. A list of the relevant Excel formulas is included in the Appendix of Excel formulas. Additionally, the Excel formulas used in the examples are presented adjacent to the results to display the underlying computations.

Typically when conducting an experiment or quasi-experiment, the goal of the research is to determine whether there are significant differences in the mean of the dependent variable across the conditions of the independent variable. There are several quantitative analyses designed to compare mean differences, and the choice of the test depends on the number of conditions of the independent variable (two or more than two), the design of the study (within-subjects or between-subjects design) and the number of independent variables (one or more than one). All of these analyses assume that the dependent variable data is measured on an interval or ratio scale. In these analyses, the data on the independent variable is either measured on a nominal or ordinal scale.

We will begin by discussing quantitative analyses that are designed for hypotheses that only involve the comparison of two groups or two levels of the independent variable (*t*-tests). In general, the formulas for *t*-tests involve computing a ratio of the observed difference between the means to the expected difference between the means. The expected difference between the means is based on the estimated standard error, which tells on average how far any sample mean will deviate from the population mean. Said otherwise, it is the deviance expected due to sampling error. The larger the ratio of the actual difference to the expected difference, the more likely we are able to say that two means are significantly different.

Next, we explain the appropriate class of tests that should be used when there are more than two levels of the independent variable (F-tests or ANOVAs). Lastly, we explain analyses with more than one independent variable (factorial ANOVAs). In general, the conceptual basis of the ANOVA formula is a computed ratio of the average variance between conditions or groups of the independent variable to the average variance within each group (also known as error variance). As the value of this ratio increases, the more likely we are to say that there is at least one difference between the means associated with each group. Recall that inferential quantitative analyses use samples to make inferences about a population. For this reason, null hypotheses posed in inferential tests are focused on the population although they are tested with samples.

Independent t-tests

When the design of the study is between-subjects (see Chapter 3) and only two conditions or levels of the independent variable are being compared, the dependent variable is measured using an interval or ratio measurement scale, and the assumptions of parametric tests are met, an independent t-test is appropriate. In studies of this nature, the researcher uses two samples to represent two populations and employs quantitative analyses on the samples to test hypotheses about these populations being significantly different from each other.

The null hypothesis is that the mean of the population from condition 1 is the same as the mean of the population with condition 2:

$$H_o: \mu_{condition\ 1} = \mu_{condition\ 2}$$

If the analysis is statistically significant, one rejects the null hypothesis and concludes that the mean of the population from which sample 1 was selected is significantly different from the mean of the population from which sample 2 was selected. Otherwise, one fails to reject the null hypothesis and concludes that there is not enough evidence to suggest that the mean of the population from which sample 1 was selected is significantly different from the mean of the population from which sample 2 was selected. The independent t-test uses the t-distribution to determine the probability associated with the observed test result. The t-distribution changes shape based on degrees of freedom. Degrees of freedom (abbreviated df) refer to the number of values that are free to vary in a calculation. As a simple example of the concept, consider the calculation of a mean. If the mean of three scores is 10 and we know that two of the scores are 7 and 15, we are left with no degrees of freedom (or values that can vary) as the third score must be 8. All of the quantitative analyses covered in this book include an associated degree of freedom as each of them constrains some of the values in the data in the process of computing the test. For example, many tests require that the mean be computed, which constrains at least one of the numbers for a given variable. The specific formula depends on how many values are free to vary when computing the components of the formula for the quantitative analysis.

The formula for an independent t-test is as follows:

$$t_{obtained} = \frac{(M_1 - M_2) - (\mu_1 - \mu_2)}{S_{(M_1 - M_2)}}$$
Eq. 4.4

$$S_{(M_1 - M_2)} = \sqrt{\frac{s_p^2}{n_1} + \frac{s_p^2}{n_2}}$$
Eq. 4.5

$$\frac{((n_1 - 1) * s_1^2) + ((n_2 - 1) * s_2^2)}{(n_1 - 1) + (n_2 - 1)}$$
Eq. 4.6

where M_1 is the mean of the sample for condition 1, M_2 is the mean of the sample for condition 2, μ_1 is the mean of the population for condition 1, μ_1 is the mean of the population for condition 2, $S_{(M_1 - M_2)}$ is the estimated standard error of the difference between sample means, s_p^2 is the pooled variance between the two samples, n_1 is the size of the sample in condition 1, n_2 is the size of the sample in condition 2, s_1^2 is the variance of the sample in condition 1, and s_2^2 is the variance of the sample in condition 2. The total degrees of freedom for an independent t-test are $n_1 n_2 - 2$.

A few specifics about the formula warrant further discussion. First, notice that the numerator includes the term $\mu_1 - \mu_2$. This value will always be equal to 0, per the null hypothesis (if the two means are equal, their difference is 0). Thus, this term can effectively be eliminated from the equation. Second, because the focus of this test is the difference between two means, one compares that difference to the estimated difference between any two sample means.

Because the standard error of the difference between means (Eq. 4.5) involves two sample means, we must combine the variability associated with both of these means. However, the two samples may have different variances (particularly if they have different sample sizes). Because larger samples tend to be a better estimator of the population (by definition, a larger sample is a closer approximation of the population), this sample should be weighted more heavily in the calculations. This is precisely what is done in the formula for the pooled variance (Eq. 4.6). This formula is essentially calculating a weighted mean of the two sample variances. Note that if the samples are of the same size, this is the same as calculating a regular mean, as both are weighted equally. Next, once the pooled variance is estimated we use this value to calculate the estimated standard error of the difference between means (Eq. 4.5), which involves dividing the pooled variance by the sample size for each sample. The steps involved in computing an independent t-test are summarized in Table 4.3.

Table 4.3 Steps to calculating an independent t-test

---

1. State the null hypothesis
2. Calculate M_1 and M_2
3. Calculate S_1^2 and S_2^2
4. Calculate S_p^2
5. Calculate $S_{(M_1 - M_2)}$
6. Calculate $t_{obtained}$
7. Determine the probability associated with $t_{obtained}$
8. Make a decision to reject or fail to reject the null hypothesis
9. Interpret the decision

Box 4.6 Conducting an independent t-test

Kite Incorporated wants to improve its customer service experience. The company designs two training programs to help customer service representatives improve customer satisfaction. One of the training programs is entirely online and the other is in-person training. The company wants to know which of the training programs is more effective. To test this question, 14 customer service employees undergo the in-person training and their customer service scores are recorded two weeks later. A group of 14 employees undergoes the online training. Their customer service scores are also recorded. The customer service scores are rated on a 10-point rating scale, with 10 representing the highest level of service, and are based on customer reports.

Step 1: State the null hypothesis. The null hypothesis is that the mean customer service rating of the population of those who undergo the online training is the same as the mean customer service rating of the population of those who undergo the in-person training:

$$Ho: \mu_{online\ training} = \mu_{in-person\ training} \text{ or}$$

$$Ho: \mu_{online\ training} - \mu_{in-person\ training} = 0$$

Recall that the null hypothesis focuses on the population, but we use a sample to test the hypothesis and then make inferences about the population.

Step 2: Calculate M_1 and M_2. The means can be computed using Eq. 4.2 and the 'average' formula in Excel.

Step 3: Calculate S_1^2 and S_2^2. The variance can be computed using Eq. 4.3 and the 'var.s' function in Excel.

	A	B	C	D	E	F
1	Online	In-Person				
2	6	8		Online		
3	7	6		$M =$	6.86	=AVERAGE(A2:A15)
4	6	5		$S^2 =$	1.67	=VAR.S(A2:A15)
5	5	8				
6	9	9		In-Person		
7	7	10		$M =$	7.71	=AVERAGE(B2:B15)
8	5	10		$S^2 =$	3.30	=VAR.S(B2:B15)
9	8	8				
10	7	9		Pooled variance =	2.48	=(((14-1)*E4)+((14-1)*E8))/((14-1)+(14-1))
11	9	6		Standard error =	0.60	=SQRT((E10/14)+(E10/14))
12	8	5		$t =$	1.44	=(E7-E3)/E11
13	6	8		df =	26	=COUNT(A2:B15)-2
14	7	10		probability of $t =$	0.16	=T.TEST(A2:A15, B2:B15, 2,3)
15	6	6				

Step 4: Calculate s_p^2. The pooled variance is computed using Eq. 4.6:

$$s_p^2 = \frac{(14-1)*1.67+(14-1)*3.30}{(14-1)+(14-1)} = 2.48$$

Step 5: Calculate $S_{(M_1-M_2)}$. The standard error of the difference in the means is computed using Eq. 4.5:

$$S_{(M_1-M_2)} = \sqrt{\frac{2.48}{14}+\frac{2.48}{14}} = 0.60$$

Step 6: Calculate $t_{obtained}$. Eq. 4.4 is used to compute the t-test:

$$t_{obtained} = \frac{(7.71-6.86)-(0)}{.60} = 1.44$$

Step 7: Determine the probability associated with $t_{obtained}$. The probability associated with a $t = |1.44|$ is 0.16. This can be determined using the exact probability in a statistics program or using the critical value of 2.056 which is the t-value associated with 26 df and a probability of 0.05. The significance of the t-value can be assessed using the 't.test' function = t.test(data from online condition, data from in person condition, 2, 3) where the '2' in the formula stands for number of tails for the test (two-tailed) and the '3' in the formula indicates the type of t-test (independent with unequal variances assumed).

Step 8: Make a decision to reject or fail to reject the null hypothesis. Based on the results of the t-test, we fail to reject the null hypothesis.

Step 9: Interpret the decision. There is no evidence of statistically significant differences between the two training programs. From a practical standpoint, Kite Incorporated should consider implementing the online training because it is likely less expensive to administer than the in-person training, and there is no evidence of differences in effectiveness between the two types of training.

Paired t-tests

When the design of the study is within-subjects (see Chapter 3), only two conditions or levels of the independent variable are being compared, the dependent variable is measured using an interval or ratio measurement scale and the assumptions of parametric tests are met, a paired t-test is appropriate. In studies of this nature, the researcher is focused on two conditions of the independent variable but tests both conditions using a single sample of participants that is exposed to both conditions. In this sense, each participant serves as their own referent. The focus of the paired t-test is to determine whether the sample mean difference score (the average difference across participants when the score on one condition is subtracted from the other) as a representative of the population difference score is significantly different from zero.

The null hypothesis for this test is that the mean difference score in the population is equal to zero:

$$H_o : \mu_D = 0$$

If the result is statistically significant, one rejects the null hypothesis and concludes that the mean difference score in the population is significantly different from zero. Otherwise, one fails to reject it and concludes that there is not enough evidence to suggest that the mean difference score in the population is significantly different from zero. The paired t-test uses the t-distribution to determine the probability associated with the observed test result.

The formula for a paired t-test is:

$$t_{obtained} = \frac{M_D - \mu_D}{S_{M_D}}$$
Eq. 4.7

$$S_{M_D} = \sqrt{\frac{S_D^2}{n_D}}$$
Eq. 4.8

$$D = X_2 - X_1$$
Eq. 4.9

where D is the difference score for a single participant, M_D is the mean of the difference scores across all participants in the sample, μ_D is the mean difference score of the population as specified by the null hypothesis, S_{M_D} is the estimated standard error of the mean difference scores, S_D^2 is the variance of the difference scores in the sample and n_D is the number of difference scores in the sample (this is identical to the number of participants if all participants are exposed to both conditions). The total degrees of freedom for a paired t-test are $n_D - 1$. The steps involved in computing a paired t-test are summarized in Table 4.4.

Table 4.4   Steps to calculating a paired t-test

1. State the null hypothesis
2. Calculate D for each individual
3. Calculate M_D
4. Calculate S_D^2
5. Calculate S_{M_D}
6. Compute $t_{obtained}$
7. Determine the probability associated with $t_{obtained}$
8. Make a decision to reject or fail to reject the null hypothesis
9. Interpret the decision

Box 4.7   Conducting a paired t-test

Piranha Brands is interested in increasing customer awareness of its new environmentally sustainable household cleaning products. The company administers a survey to 13 customers about their awareness of these new products and records their responses. These 13 customers are subsequently sent advertising materials about the new cleaning products. Two weeks later, these customers complete a second survey about their awareness of the new products. Piranha wants to know if the advertising campaign is worth administering to all of its customers. In other words, are the post-advertising awareness scores significantly higher than the pre-advertising scores?

Step 1: State the null hypothesis. The difference between the pre- and post-advertising awareness scores in the population will be zero:

$$H_o : \mu_D = 0$$

Recall that the null hypothesis focuses on the population, but we use a sample to test the hypothesis and then make inferences about the population.

Step 2: Calculate D for each individual. The difference score is calculated using Eq. 4.9 for each individual.

Step 3: Calculate M_D. M_D is calculated by computing the means of the difference scores calculated in step 2. This can be done using Eq. 4.2 or in Excel using the 'average' function. The differences scores must first be computed and then averaged; averaging the scores for the pre-advertising and then averaging the

(Continued)

(Continued)

scores for the post-advertising and subtracting those two values will give a different and incorrect M_D.

Step 4: Calculate S_D^2. This is calculated using Eq. 4.3 and the 'var.s' function in Excel. Note that the calculations involve only the variance of the D scores for each participant. The pre- and post-advertising scores are not used in any of the calculations after D is calculated.

	A	B	C	D	E	F	G	H
1	Pre	Post	Difference Score					
2	2	5	3	=B2 - A2				
3	2	4	2	=B3 - A3				
4	4	5	1	=B4 - A4				
5	1	5	4	=B5 - A5		M_D =		2.85 =average(C2:C14)
6	3	5	2	=B6 - A6		S_D^2 =		1.31 =var.s(C2:C14)
7	1	5	4	=B7 - A7		S_{M_D} =		0.32 =SQRT(G6/13)
8	1	5	4	=B8 - A8				
9	1	4	3	=B9 - A9				
10	1	3	2	=B10 - A10		t =		8.97 =G5/G7
11	3	4	1	=B11 - A11		df =		12 =COUNT(C2:C14)-1
12	2	5	3	=B12 - A12		probability of t =		0.000 =T.TEST(A2:A14,B2:B14, 2,1)
13	1	5	4	=B13 - A13				
14	1	5	4	=B14 - A14				

Step 5: Calculate S_{M_D}. The value of S_{M_D} is computed using Eq. 4.8:

$$S_{M_D} = \sqrt{\frac{1.31}{13}} = 0.32$$

Note that because each participant completed the pre- and post-advertising survey, n_D is identical to the number of participants in the sample. It is common in within-subjects designs to have some attrition, particularly if the study takes place over a long period of time. In this case, only participants who complete both measurement points are included in calculations.

Step 6: Compute the $t_{obtained}$. The t-test is computed using Eq. 4.7:

$$t_{obtained} = \frac{2.85 - 0}{.32} = 8.97$$

Note that the value of μ_D comes from what is specified in the null hypothesis (0).

Step 7: Determine the probability associated with the $t_{obtained}$. The probability associated with the $t = |8.97|$ is < 0.001. This can be determined using the exact probability in a statistics program or using the critical value of 2.179 which is the *t*-value associated with 12 *df* and a probability of 0.05. This can be done in Excel using the 't.test' function: = t.test(data from online condition, data from in person condition, 2, 1) where the '2' in the formula stands for number of tails for the test (two-tailed) and the '1' in the formula indicates the type of *t*-test (paired).

Step 8: Make a decision to reject or fail to reject the null hypothesis. Given the test result, the null hypothesis is rejected.

Step 9: Interpret the decision. Piranha should consider implementing the advertising with all of their customers. There was a statistically significant increase in awareness of the new environmentally sustainable household cleaning products after the advertising.

Single-factor independent analysis of variance (ANOVA)

When the design of the study is between-subjects (see Chapter 3) and more than two conditions or levels of the independent variable are being compared, the dependent variable is measured using an interval or ratio measurement scale, and the assumptions of parametric tests are met, a single-factor independent ANOVA is appropriate. In studies of this nature, the researcher uses at least three samples (referred to later as groups for ease of interpretation) to represent at least three populations and employs quantitative analysis to determine whether there is at least one significant difference between the populations. Post hoc tests are used to determine the precise nature of the significant differences.

The null hypothesis for this analysis is that there are no significant differences among the *k* populations:

$$H_o : \mu_1 = \mu_2 = \mu_3 = ... = \mu_k$$

If the result is statistically significant, one rejects the null hypothesis and concludes that at least one of the comparisons demonstrates a mean difference in the population that is significantly different from zero. Otherwise, one fails to reject the null hypothesis and concludes that there is not enough evidence to suggest that there are any mean differences in the population that are significantly different from zero. This test is called an omnibus test as it indicates that there is a difference, but not the specific comparison where it exists. The ANOVA uses the *F*-distribution to determine the probability associated with the observed test result.

The formula for a single-factor independent ANOVA is:

$$F = \frac{MS_{between}}{MS_{within}}$$

Eq. 4.10

$$MS_{between} = \frac{\Sigma n_i * (M_i - M_G)^2}{k-1}$$

Eq. 4.11

$$MS_{within} = \frac{\Sigma s_i^2}{k}$$

Eq. 4.12

where $MS_{between}$ is the mean square (average variance) between groups, MS_{within} is the mean square (average variance) within each group, n_i is the size of the sample for a given group i, M_i is the mean of a given group i, M_G is the grand mean of all par-ticipants in the study (all groups combined), k is the number of groups and s_i^2 is the variance of given group i. Note that the term groups is synonymous with conditions in the study or levels of the independent variable. The formulas are $df_{between} = k - 1$ and $df_{within} = n_T - k$, where n_T is the total sample size across all groups.

In cases where the null hypothesis is rejected, post hoc tests are conducted to determine exactly where the significant differences lie (i.e. is group 1 different from all other groups or just different from group 2?). There are many types of post hoc tests with different advantages and drawbacks. Some examples include the Tukey-Kramer, Brown-Fosythe, Sheffe's test, Duncan's Multiple Range test, Newman-Keuls test and Tukey's Honestly Significant Difference (HSD) test (see Winer et al., 1991 for a full discussion of post hoc tests). One major differentiator between the tests is their level of conservatism (i.e. how likely one is to reject the null hypothesis). The process of conducting post hoc tests first involves calculating the post hoc test value. This value is compared to the absolute value of the mean difference between each unique comparison of groups. For each comparison, if the mean difference exceeds the test value, the groups are considered statistically significantly different. If the mean dif-ference is less than the test value, the groups are not significantly different. When the overall F is significant, at least one of the post hoc comparisons should be significant. Tukey's HSD test is considered in more detail as it is a commonly used test and one of the more conservative post hoc tests. The formula for Tukey's HSD is:

$$HSD = q * \sqrt{\frac{MS_{within}}{n_i}}$$

Eq. 4.13

where q can be found by using the q-critical table found in most statistics textbooks and on the internet, which requires k and df_{within} (i.e. $n_T - k$). In cases where n_i is not identical across groups, a harmonic mean must be calculated using the formula:

$$n = \frac{k}{\dfrac{1}{n_1} + \dfrac{1}{n_2} + \dfrac{1}{n_3} + ... + \dfrac{1}{n_k}}$$

Eq. 4.14

The steps involved in computing a single-factor independent ANOVA are summarized in Table 4.5.

Table 4.5 Steps to calculating a single-factor independent ANOVA

1. State the null hypothesis
2. Calculate M for each group
3. Calculate M_G
4. Calculate $MS_{between}$
5. Calculate s^2 for each group
6. Calculate MS_{within}
7. Calculate $F_{obtained}$
8. Determine the probability associated with $F_{obtained}$
9. Make a decision to reject or fail to reject the null hypothesis
10. In cases where the null hypothesis is rejected, decide which post hoc test to use
11. When using Tukey's HSD, locate q
12. Calculate Tukey's HSD
13. Compare the HSD value to the absolute value of the mean difference between each group
14. Interpret the results

Box 4.8   Conducting a single-factor independent ANOVA

Kite Incorporated wants to improve its customer service experience. The company designs two training programs to help customer service representatives improve customer satisfaction. One of the training programs is entirely online and the other is in-person training. The company wants to know if the training programs are effective compared to a group who gets no training (i.e. a control group). To test this question, 40 customer service employees undergo the in-person training and their customer service scores are recorded two weeks later. A group of 36 employees undergoes the online training. Their customer service scores are also recorded. The control group consists of 38 employees, who do not undergo any training. The customer service scores are based on customer reports and are rated on a 10-point rating scale, with 10 representing the highest level of service. The mean customer service score for the sample of participants who underwent in-person training was 7.50 with a variance of 1.25, the mean customer service score for participants who underwent the online training was 7.25 with a variance of 1.75, and the mean customer service score for the control group was 6.80 with a variance of 1.00.

Step 1: State the null hypothesis. The null hypothesis is that there are no significant differences among the three populations:

$$H_0 : \mu_{in-person\ training} = \mu_{online\ training} = \mu_{control}$$

(Continued)

(Continued)

Recall that the null hypothesis focuses on the populations, but we use samples to test the hypothesis and then make inferences about the populations.

Step 2: Calculate M for each group. We will not need to calculate these because they are given: 7.5, 7.25 and 6.8. In many cases, one may be given raw data from the sample and would then calculate the means using the formula presented in Eq. 4.2 and the 'average' function in Excel.

Step 3: Calculate M_G. There are multiple ways to calculate M_G. If one is given the raw data, one can simply sum all of the values and divide by the total N. If one is only given the group means rather than the raw data, as is the case in this example, a weighted mean must be used to calculate the overall mean. The means are weighted by their sample. Note that if the sample sizes for each group are the same, a simple mean of the means can be computed. This can be done in Excel by manually entering the formula for a weighted mean:

$$M_G = \frac{40*7.50 + 36*7.25 + 38*6.80}{40 + 36 + 38} = 7.19$$

	A	B	C	D	E	F	G
1		Control		Online		In-person	
2	$M =$	6.80	$M =$	7.25	$M =$	7.50	
3	$s^2 =$	1.00	$s^2 =$	1.75	$s^2 =$	1.25	
4	$N =$	38	$N =$	36	$N =$	40	
5							
6	Grand mean =	7.19	=((B2*B4)+(D2*D4)+(F2*F4))/(B4+D4+F4)				
7							
8	MS Between =	4.88	=((B4*(B2-B8)^2)+(D4*(D2-B8)^2)+(F4*(F2-B8)^2))/(F13-1)				
9	MS Within =	1.33	=(SUM(B3,D3,F3)/(F13))				
10	F for training =	3.66	=B8/B9				
11	Probability of F =	0.03	=F.DIST.RT(B10,F14,F15)				
12							
13	$q =$	3.36			$k =$	3.00	
14	HSD =	0.63	=B13*(SQRT(B9/F16))	df between =	2.00	=F13-1	
15				df within =	111.00	=(SUM(B4,D4,F4)-F13)	
16	$M_{in-person} - M_{online} =$	0.25	=ABS(F2-D2)	Harmonic Mean =	37.93	=(F13/((1/B4)+(1/D4)+(1/F4)))	
17	$M_{in-person} - M_{control} =$	0.70	=ABS(F2-B2)				
18	$M_{online} - M_{control} =$	0.45	=ABS(D2-B2)				
19							

Step 4: Calculate $MS_{between}$. Next, the value of $MS_{between}$ is computed using Eq. 4.11. This is done in Excel by manually entering the formula in Eq. 4.11:

$$MS_{between} = \frac{38*(6.80 - 7.19)^2 + 36*(7.25 - 7.19)^2 + 40*(7.50 - 7.19)^2}{2} = 4.88$$

Step 5: Calculate s^2 for each group. We will not need to calculate these because they are given as 1.25, 1.75 and 1.00. These were calculated using Eq. 4.3 or can be calculated in Excel using the 'var.s' function: = var.s (in-person); = var.s (online); = var.s (control).

Step 6: Calculate MS_{within}. Using Eq. 4.12, the value of MS_{within} is computed. This is done in Excel by manually entering the formula in Eq. 4.12:

$$MS_{within} = \frac{1.25 + 1.75 + 1}{3} = 1.33$$

Step 7: Calculate $F_{obtained}$. Using Eq. 4.10, the value of F is computed. This is done in Excel by manually entering the formula in Eq. 4.10:

$$F = \frac{4.88}{1.33} = 3.66$$

Step 8: Determine the probability associated with $F_{obtained}$. The probability associated with $F = 3.66$ is 0.03. This can be determined using the exact probability in a statistics program or using the critical value of 3.08 which is the F-value associated with a df of 2, 111 and a probability of 0.05. This is done in Excel by using the 'f.dist.rt' function: =f.dist.rt(F-value, df between, df within).

Step 9: Make a decision to reject or fail to reject null hypothesis. Based on the results, one rejects the null hypothesis. There is at least one difference among the groups.

Step 10: In cases where the null hypothesis is rejected, decide which post hoc test to use. For this example, we show the results of Tukey's HSD test.

Step 11: When using Tukey's HSD, locate q. One can find the value of q using a q-critical table found in most statistics textbooks and on the internet. In this case, $q = 3.36$ based on k of 3, df_{within} of 111 and an alpha of 0.05.

Step 12: Calculate Tukey's HSD. Using the values from the previous steps, the harmonic mean can be computed using Eq. 4.15. Next, the HSD can be computed using Eq. 4.13. This is done in Excel by manually computing the formula given in Eqs 4.13 and 4.15:

$$n = \frac{3}{\frac{1}{40} + \frac{1}{36} + \frac{1}{38}} = 37.93$$

$$HSD = 3.36 * \sqrt{\frac{1.33}{37.93}} = .63$$

(Continued)

(Continued)

Step 13: Compare the HSD value to the absolute value of the mean difference between each group. Next, each possible comparison is made. These formula must be manually entered into Excel using subtraction and absolute value ('abs') functions =abs(mean of in person – mean of online), etc.:

$$M_{in\ person} - M_{online} = 7.50 - 7.25 = 0.25$$

|0.25| < 0.63 therefore these two groups are not statistically significantly different from each other:

$$M_{in\ person} - M_{control} = 7.50 - 6.80 = 0.70$$

|0.70| > 0.63 therefore these two groups are statistically significantly different from each other:

$$M_{online} - M_{control} = 7.25 - 6.80 = 0.45$$

|0.45| < 0.63 therefore these two groups are not statistically significantly different from each other.

Step 14: Interpret the results. Participants in the in-person training condition had significantly higher customer service scores than participants in the control group; however, the in person scores did not significantly differ from participants in the online training. There were also no significant differences between the online training and the control group. The organization should consider implementing the in-person training, as it significantly increased customer service scores.

Single-factor repeated-measures analysis of variance (ANOVA)

When the design of the study is within-subjects and more than two conditions or levels of the independent variable are being compared, and the dependent variable is measured using an interval or ratio measurement scale, a single-factor repeated-measures ANOVA is appropriate. In addition to the assumptions of parametric tests, there is an additional assumption of sphericity for this test, which means that the variances of the repeated measures are equal, and the correlations among the repeated measures are equal. If this assumption is violated, the test can still be conducted but requires certain adjustments to the formula listed below.

In studies of this nature, the researcher is focused on at least three conditions of the independent variable but tests these conditions using a single sample of participants that is exposed to all conditions. In this sense, each participant serves as his or her own referent. The focus of the repeated-measures ANOVA is to determine if there is at least one significant difference between the populations that are represented by the samples. Post hoc tests are used to determine the precise nature of the significant differences. Note that only participants who are exposed to all conditions in the study should be included in analyses. Participants with missing data should be excluded.

The null hypothesis is that there are no significant differences among the k populations:

$$H_0 : \mu_1 = \mu_2 = \mu_3 = ... = \mu_k$$

If the result is statistically significant, one rejects the null hypothesis and concludes that there is at least one difference between the population means. Otherwise, one fails to reject the null hypothesis and concludes that there is not enough evidence to suggest that there is at least one difference between the population means. The single-factor repeated-measures ANOVA uses the F-distribution to determine the probability associated with the observed test result.

Conceptually, a single-factor repeated-measures ANOVA is similar to a single-factor independent ANOVA. The formula computes a ratio of the average variance between measurement periods to the average variance within each measurement period. The numerator of the ratio is identical to that in the formula for a single-factor independent ANOVA. The difference lies in the denominator.

The denominator of the repeated-measures ANOVA formula incorporates what is labelled the 'residual variance' rather than 'within-subjects variance'. The formula for computing residual variance involves calculating the within-subjects variance and then subtracting out the 'subjects variance'. What is left over is the residual variance (consider the meaning of the term residual - it means left over). It is important to take this extra step in the repeated-measures ANOVA because the same participants, or subjects, are included in each measurement point. Therefore, some of the variance within each group will be constant across measurement points (i.e. a person who scores the highest on a leadership assessment at time 1 is likely to also be at the top of the distribution at time 2 and time 3). The F statistic is only concerned with error that is random and not systematic (i.e. consistent across conditions), so one must subtract this systematic variance attributed to subjects out of the equation. Once this is done, the interpretation of a single-factor repeated-measures ANOVA is similar to that of an independent ANOVA.

The formula for a single-factor repeated-measures ANOVA is:

$$F = \frac{MS_{between}}{MS_{residual}}$$

Eq. 4.15

$$MS_{between} = \frac{\Sigma n_{subjects} * (M_i - M_G)^2}{k - 1}$$

Eq. 4.16

$$MS_{residual} = \frac{((n_{subjects} - 1)*(\Sigma s_i^2)) - (k*(\Sigma(M_{subject} - M_G)^2))}{(n_{subjects} - 1)*(k-1)}$$ Eq. 4.17

where $MS_{between}$ is the mean square (average variance) between groups, $MS_{residual}$ is the mean square (average variance) within each group with the variance associated with each individual parcelled out, $n_{subjects}$ is the number of participants in the study, M_i is the mean of a given condition i, M_G is the grand mean of all participants in the study (all conditions combined), k is the number of groups, s_i^2 is the variance of a given group i, and $M_{subject}$ is the mean score for a participant across all conditions. The formulas are $df_{between} = k - 1$ and $df_{residual} = (n_{subjects} - 1)*(k-1)$.

In cases where the null hypothesis is rejected, post hoc tests are typically conducted to determine exactly where the significant differences lie (i.e. is time 1 different from all other time points or just different from time 2?). As discussed, there are many types of post hoc tests and this chapter will focus on Tukey's HSD test:

$$HSD = q * \sqrt{\frac{MS_{residual}}{n_i}}$$ Eq. 4.18

The steps involved in computing a single-factor repeated-measures ANOVA are summarized in Table 4.6.

Table 4.6   Steps to calculating a single-factor repeated-measures ANOVA

1. State the null hypothesis
2. Calculate M for each group
3. Calculate M_G
4. Calculate $MS_{between}$
5. Calculate s^2 for each group
6. Calculate $M_{subject}$ for each participant
7. Calculate $MS_{residual}$
8. Calculate $F_{obtained}$
9. Determine the probability associated with $F_{obtained}$
10. Make a decision to reject or fail to reject the null hypothesis
11. In cases where the null hypothesis is rejected, decide which post-hoc test to use
12. If using Tukey's HSD, locate q
13. Compute Tukey's HSD
14. Compare the HSD value to the absolute value of the mean difference between each group
15. Interpret the results

Box 4.9   Conducting a repeated-measures ANOVA

Piranha Brands is interested in tracking customer satisfaction with three brands of household cleaning products. The company distributes free samples of their 'extra strength' household cleaning products to 10 customers and also sends these customers a survey asking about their satisfaction with the extra strength product. Two weeks later, Piranha sends the same group of 10 customers a second brand of cleaning product from the environmentally sustainable product line. The customers are asked to rate their satisfaction with the environmentally sustainable product. Finally, two weeks later, the 10 customers are sent a third sample, of a new odourless cleaning product. The customers also rate their satisfaction with this product. In summary, the 10 customers try three different cleaning products and rate their satisfaction with each product. The satisfaction scores range from 1 to 100. Piranha is considering removing one of their three brands from the market based on customer preferences. Using the customer satisfaction scores, they will determine whether there is a product that consumers are significantly less satisfied with than the others.

Note: For illustration purposes, a small sample size of 10 is used in this example. We advise using larger samples when actually conducting research.

Step 1: State the null hypothesis. The null hypothesis is that there are no significant differences among the three populations:

$$H_0: \mu_{extra\ strength} = \mu_{environment} = \mu_{odourless}$$

Recall that although the null hypothesis is focused on the population, we use sample data to test the hypothesis and make inferences about the population.

Step 2: Calculate M for each group. These were calculated using the formula presented in Eq. 4.2 or the 'average' function in Excel. $M_{extra\ strength} = 66.40$, $M_{environment} = 77.30$, $M_{odourless} = 74.30$.

Step 3: Calculate M_G. With this design, the sample sizes for each group will always be the same as it is the same individuals in each group. Thus, M_G can be calculated by adding the M for each condition and dividing by the number of conditions. Alternatively, it can be computed by summing all data points and dividing by the number of data points. This is computed in Excel using the 'average' function = average (all ratings):

$$M_G = \frac{66.4 + 77.3 + 74.3}{3} = 72.67$$

(Continued)

(Continued)

	Customer ID	Extra Strength		Environmentally Sustainable		Odourless		$M_{Subject}$	
1									
2	1	50		79		71		66.67	=average(C2:G2)
3	2	43		92		88		74.33	=average(C3:G3)
4	3	62		69		63		64.67	=average(C4:G4)
5	4	58		65		60		61.00	=average(C5:G5)
6	5	60		59		57		58.67	=average(C6:G6)
7	6	62		79		69		70.00	=average(C7:G7)
8	7	78		87		85		83.33	=average(C8:G8)
9	8	92		84		93		89.67	=average(C9:G9)
10	9	81		81		79		80.33	=average(C10:G10)
11	10	78		78		78		78.00	=average(C11:G11)
12		$M_{Environ. Sustain.}$ = 66.40		$M_{Environ. Sustain.}$ = 77.30		$M_{Odourless}$ = 74.30			
13		=average(C2:C11)		=average(E2:E11)		=average(G2:G11)			
15		$S^2_{Environ. Sustain.}$ = 233.82		$S^2_{Environ. Sustain.}$ = 103.34		$S^2_{Odourless}$ = 150.90			
16		=var.s(C2:C11)		=var.s(E2:E11)		=var.s(G2:G11)			
18	N= 10		k=	3					
19	df between= 2	=E18-1		df resid=	18	=(B18-1)*(E18-1)			

	A	B	C
21	Grand Mean =	72.67	=average(C2:G11)
22	MS Between=	317.03	=((B18*(C12-B21)^2) +(B18*(E12-B21)^2) + (B18*(G12-B21)^2)) /2
23	MS Residual =	88.70	=(((B18-1)*(C15+E15+G15))-(((I2-B21)^2+(I3-B21)^2+(I4-B21)^2+(I5-B21)^2+(I6-B21)^2 +(I7-B21)^2+(I8-B21)^2+(I9-B21)^2+(I10-B21)^2+(I11-B21)^2)*E18))/((B18-1)*(E18-1))
24	F =	3.57	=B22/B23
25	Probability of F =	0.049	=F.DIST.RT(B24,B19,E19)
27	q =	3.61	
28	HSD =	10.75	=B27*(SQRT((B23/B18)))
30	$M_{extra strength}$- $M_{environmentally sustainable}$ =	10.90	=ABS(C12-E12)
31	$M_{extra strength}$- $M_{odourless}$ =	7.90	=ABS(C12-G12)
32	$M_{environmentally sustainable}$- $M_{odourless}$ =	3.00	=ABS(E12-G12)

Step 4: Calculate $MS_{between}$. Using Eq. 4.16, the $MS_{between}$ is computed. This is computed in Excel by manually entering the formula from Eq. 4.16:

$$MS_{between} = \frac{10*(66.4-72.7)^2 +10*(77.3-72.7)^2 +10*(74.3-72.7)^2}{2} = 317.03$$

Step 5: Calculate s^2 for each group. Variances are calculated using Eq. 4.3 or can be calculated in Excel using the 'vars' function = variance (ratings for extra strength); = variance (ratings for environmentally sustainable); = variance (ratings for odourless). $S^2_{extra strength}$ = 233.82, $S^2_{environment}$ = 103.34, $S^2_{odourless}$ = 150.90.

Step 6: Calculate $M_{subject}$ for each participant. The $M_{subject}$ is calculated by averaging each participant's scores across the various conditions using Eq. 4.2. These values are listed in the $M_{subject}$ column in the Excel screenshot. This is calculated in Excel using the 'average' function = average (customer 1 ratings); = average (customer 2 ratings); = average (customer 3 ratings), etc.

Step 7: Calculate $MS_{residual}$. Using Eq. 4.17, the $MS_{residual}$ is computed. This is calculated in Excel by manually entering the formula for Eq. 4.17:

$$\sum s_i^2 = 233.82 + 103.34 + 150.90 = 488.07$$

$$\sum(M_{subject} - M_G)^2 = (66.67 - 72.67)^2 + (74.33 - 72.67)^2 + (64.67 - 72.67)^2 +$$
$$(61.00 - 72.67)^2 + (58.67 - 72.67)^2 + (70.00 - 72.67)^2 +$$
$$(83.33 - 72.67)^2 + (89.67 - 72.67)^2 + (80.33 - 72.67)^2 +$$
$$(7.80 - 72.67)^2 = 932$$

$$MS_{residual} = \frac{9 * 488.07 - 3 * 932}{9 * 2} = 88.70$$

Step 8: Calculate $F_{obtained}$. Using Eq. 4.15, the $F_{obtained}$ is computed. This is calculated in Excel by manually entering the formula for Eq. 4.15:

$$F = \frac{317.03}{88.7} = 3.57$$

Step 9: Determine the probability associated with the $F_{obtained}$. The probability associated with the $F = 3.57$ is 0.049. This can be determined using the exact probability in a statistics program or using the critical value of 3.55 which is the F-value associated with df of 2, 18 and a probability of 0.05. This is calculated in Excel using the 'f.dist.rt' function = f.dist.rt(F-value, df between, df residual).

Step 10: Make a decision to reject or fail to reject the null hypothesis. In this case, we reject the null hypothesis. There is at least one difference among the groups.

Step 11: In cases where the null hypothesis is rejected, decide which post hoc test to use. For this example, we show the results of Tukey's HSD test.

Step 12: If using Tukey's HSD, locate q. One can find the value of q using a q-critical table found in most statistics textbooks and on the internet. Based on k of 3, $df_{residual}$ of 18 and an alpha of 0.05, q is 3.61.

Step 13: Compute Tukey's HSD. HSD can be computed using Eq. 4.18. This formula must be manually entered into Excel using Eq. 4.18:

$$HSD = 3.61 * \sqrt{\frac{88.70}{10}} = 10.75$$

Step 14: Compare the HSD value to the absolute value of the mean difference between each group. Next, each possible comparison is made. These formulas must be manually entered into Excel using subtraction and absolute value ('abs') functions = abs (mean of extra strength - mean of environmentally sustainable), etc.:

$$M_{extra\ strength} - M_{environmentally\ sustainable} = 66.40 - 77.30 = -10.90$$

(Continued)

(Continued)

$|-10.90| > 10.75$ therefore these two groups are statistically significantly different from each other.

$$M_{extra\ strength} - M_{odourless} = 66.40 - 74.30 = -7.90$$

$|-7.90| < 10.75$ therefore these two groups are not statistically significantly different from each other.

$$M_{environmentally\ sustainable} - M_{odourless} = 77.30 - 74.30 = 3.00$$

$3.00 < 10.75$ therefore these two groups are not statistically significantly different from each other.

Step 15: Interpret the results. The customer satisfaction ratings for the environmentally sustainable product were statistically significantly higher than those for the extra strength product. There were no significant differences between the environmentally sustainable and odourless products or the extra strength and odourless products in satisfaction ratings. Based on this data, Piranha may consider promoting the environmentally sustainable product.

Two-factor independent analysis of variance (ANOVA)

Researchers are often interested in simultaneously examining the influence of two independent variables on a dependent variable. When both independent variables are assessed using independent samples (i.e. between-subjects) and the scale of measurement of the dependent variable is interval or ratio, and the assumptions of parametric tests are met, a two-factor independent samples ANOVA should be used. Note that this test is used no matter the number of conditions of each independent variable. Two-factor independent samples ANOVA tests allow researchers to examine the influence of each independent variable on the dependent variable separately (these are referred to as main effects) and to examine how the two independent variables interact to impact on the dependent variable. Post hoc tests and graphs are used to determine the precise nature of the significant differences.

There are three separate null hypotheses for a two-factor independent samples ANOVA: (1) there are no significant differences among the k populations that represent the k levels of independent variable A; (2) there are no significant differences among the k populations that represent the k levels of independent variable B; and (3) there is no significant interaction between independent variable A and independent variable B. All of the mean differences between treatment conditions in the population can be explained by the main effects of the two independent variables:

$$H_o : \mu_{A1} = \mu_{A2} = \mu_{A3} = ... = \mu_{Ak}$$

$$H_o : \mu_{B1} = \mu_{B2} = \mu_{B3} = ... = \mu_{Bk}$$

Hypotheses involving interactions are traditionally described in text or graphics instead of symbolic notation.

If the analysis is statistically significant, one rejects the null hypothesis and concludes that there is: (1) at least one difference between the population means that represents the different levels of independent variable A; (2) and/or independent variable B; and (3) and/or that there is a significant interaction between A and B. Otherwise, one fails to reject the null hypothesis and concludes that there is not enough evidence to suggest that there is: (1) at least one difference between the population means that represents the different levels of independent variable A; (2) and/or independent variable B; and (3) and/or that there is a significant interaction between A and B. The two-factor independent samples ANOVA uses the F-distribution to determine the probability associated with the observed test result.

The formula for a balanced (i.e. equal sample sizes in each condition) two-factor independent samples ANOVA is:

$$F_A = \frac{MS_{between\ for\ A}}{MS_{within}}$$
Eq. 4.19

$$MS_{between\ for\ A} = \frac{\Sigma n_{i\ of\ A} * (M_{i\ of\ A} - M_G)^2}{k_A - 1}$$
Eq. 4.20

$$F_B = \frac{MS_{between\ for\ B}}{MS_{within}}$$
Eq. 4.21

$$MS_{between\ for\ B} = \frac{\Sigma n_{i\ of\ B} * (M_{i\ of\ B} - M_G)^2}{k_B - 1}$$
Eq. 4.22

$$F_{AxB} = \frac{MS_{between\ for\ AxB}}{MS_{within}}$$
Eq. 4.23

$$MS_{between\ for\ AxB} = \frac{(\Sigma n_i * (M_i - M_G)^2) - (\Sigma n_{i\ of\ A} * (M_{i\ of\ A} - M_G)^2) - (\Sigma n_{i\ of\ B} * (M_{i\ of\ B} - M_G)^2)}{(k_A - 1) * (k_B - 1)}$$
Eq. 4.24

$$MS_{within} = \frac{\Sigma s_i^2}{k}$$
Eq. 4.25

where $MS_{between\ for\ A}$ is the mean square (average variance) between groups for independent variable A, $MS_{between\ for\ B}$ is the mean square (average variance) between groups for independent variable B, $MS_{between\ for\ AxB}$ is the mean square (average variance) between groups for interaction between independent variable A and independent variable B, MS_{within} is the mean square (average variance) within each condition, n_i is the size of the sample for each condition in the study, $n_{i\ of\ A}$ is the size sample for each condition of independent variable A, $n_{i\ of\ B}$ is the size sample for each condition of independent variable B, M_i is the mean for a single condition, $M_{i\ of\ A}$ is the mean for a single condition of independent variable A, $M_{i\ of\ B}$ is the mean for a single condition of independent variable B, M_G is the grand mean of all participants in the study (all conditions combined), k is the number of conditions (or cells) in the study, k_A is the number of conditions for independent variable A, k_B is the number of conditions for independent variable B, and s_i^2 is the variance of given condition i. Note that this formula can only be used in situations where each condition in the study has the same number of participants. Slight adjustments must be made to the formula when the group sizes differ (i.e. are unbalanced). We only present this formula for the sake of brevity. The formulas for calculating degrees of freedom are $df_{between\ for\ A} = k_A - 1$, $df_{between\ for\ B} = k_B - 1$, $df_{between\ for AxB} = (k_A - 1) * (k_B - 1)$, and $df_{within} = n_T - k$, where n_T is the total sample size across all conditions.

In cases where the null hypothesis is rejected for the main effects of independent variable A and independent variable B, post hoc tests are conducted to determine exactly where the significant differences lie (i.e. is group 1 different from all other groups or just different from group 2?). The process of conducting post hoc tests in two-factor ANOVA parallels the process as it was described for single-factor independent samples ANOVA. The only difference is that two separate post hoc tests are conducted, one for each independent variable. Continuing with Tukey's HSD, the formulas become:

$$HSD = q * \sqrt{\frac{MS_{within}}{n_{iA}}}$$

Eq. 4.26

$$HSD = q * \sqrt{\frac{MS_{within}}{n_{iB}}}$$

Eq. 4.27

where q can be found by using the q-critical table found in most statistics textbooks and on the internet, which requires k_A or k_B (depending on which main effect you are conducting post hoc tests for) and df_{within}, which is equal to $N_T - k_A$ or $N_T - k_B$. n_{iA} and n_{iB} refer to the number of participants exposed to a single condition of independent variables A and B, respectively. Note that the df_{within} used for HSD is different from the df_{within} used for the overall F-tests, which incorporates both independent variables. The steps involved in computing a two-factor independent ANOVA are summarized in Table 4.7.

Table 4.7   Steps to calculating a two-factor independent ANOVA

Because there are three null hypotheses, this is divided into three iterations. One independent variable should be designated as A and the other as B before beginning the analyses.

1. State the null hypothesis for the main effect of independent variable A
2. Determine $n_{i\ of\ A}$
3. Calculate $M_{i\ for\ A}$
4. Calculate M_G
5. Determine k_A

---

6. Calculate $MS_{between\ for\ A}$

7. Calculate s^2 for each condition in the study (do not collapse across conditions of independent variable A for this - calculate s^2 for each unique condition in the study across both independent variables)

8. Calculate MS_{within}

9. Calculate $F_{A\ obtained}$

10. Determine the probability associated with $F_{A\ obtained}$

11. Make a decision to reject or fail to reject the null hypothesis

12. In cases where the null hypothesis is rejected, decide which post hoc test to use

13. If using Tukey's HSD, locate q

14. Calculate Tukey's HSD

15. Compare the HSD value to the absolute value of the mean difference between each group

16. Interpret the results in light of the null hypothesis for independent variable A

17. State the null hypothesis for the main effect of independent variable B

18. Follow steps 2-16 for independent variable B

19. State the null hypothesis for the interaction effect between independent variables A and B

20. Determine n_i

21. Calculate M_i

22. Refer to M_G, which was previously calculated in step 4

23. Calculate $\Sigma n_i * (M_i - M_G)^2$

24. Calculate $MS_{between\ for\ A\ x\ B}$ Note that $\Sigma n_{i\ of\ A} * (M_{i\ of\ A} - M_G)^2$ and $\Sigma n_{i\ of\ B} * (M_{i\ of\ B} - M_G)^2$ can be retrieved from previous calculations (numerators of $MS_{between\ for\ A}$ and $MS_{between\ for\ B}$)

25. Refer to MS_{within}, which was previously calculated in step 8

26. Calculate $F_{AxB\ obtained}$

27. Determine the probability associated with $F_{AxB\ obtained}$

28. Make a decision to reject or fail to reject the null hypothesis

29. In cases where the null hypothesis is rejected, plot the mean values for each condition on a graph to interpret the nature of the interaction effect

Box 4.10   Conducting a two-factor independent ANOVA

Kite Incorporated wants to improve its customer service experience. The company designs two training programs to help customer service representatives improve customer satisfaction. One of the training programs is entirely online and the other is in-person training. The company wants to know if the training programs are effective compared to a group who gets no training (i.e. a control group). To test this question, 20 customer service employees undergo the in-person training and their customer service scores are recorded two weeks later. A group of 20 employees undergoes the online training. Their customer service scores are also recorded. The customer service scores are rated on a 10-point rating scale, with 10 representing the highest level of service, and are based on customer reports. The control group

(Continued)

(Continued)

consists of 20 employees who do not undergo any training. In addition to understanding the effectiveness of the training programs, Kite wants to know whether
the training programs are of similar effectiveness for male and female employees.

**Step 1: State the null hypothesis for the main effect of independent variable A
(training program type).** The null hypothesis is that there are no significant differences in customer service scores among the three populations:

$$H_0: \mu_{in-person\ training} = \mu_{online\ training} = \mu_{control}$$

Recall that although the null hypothesis is focused on the population, we use sample data to test the hypothesis and make inferences about the population.

Step 2: Determine $n_{i\ of\ A}$. This refers to the number of participants exposed to each
condition of the training: 20 were exposed to each condition (20 participants in the
control, 20 participants in the online training and 20 participants in the in-person
training).

Step 3: Calculate $M_{i\ for\ A}$. This refers to the mean for each level of the training independent variable. It can be computed using Eq. 4.2. Because we are only given the
means for each condition broken down, we must collapse across males and females
to find the overall mean for each condition. This can be done in Excel using the
'average' function = average(means for control); = average(means for online); =
average(means for in-person):

$$M_{control} = \frac{6.80 + 6.75}{2} = 6.78$$

$$M_{online} = \frac{7.11 + 7.95}{2} = 7.53$$

$$M_{in-person} = \frac{7.50 + 7.49}{2} = 7.50$$

Step 4: Calculate M_G. This is simply the mean for all the data. It can be computed
using Eq. 4.2. Again, because sample sizes are the same for all conditions, it is possible to calculate a simple mean of the means. In cases of different sample sizes, a
weighted mean is necessary using the sample size of each group to weight its respective mean. This can be done in Excel using the 'average' function = average(all means):

$$M_G = \frac{6.80 + 7.11 + 7.50 + 6.75 + 7.95 + 7.49}{6} = 7.27$$

	A	B	C	D	E	F	G	H	I	J
1			Control		Online		In-person			
2		$M=$	6.80	$M=$	7.11	$M=$	7.50	$M_{male}=$	7.14	=AVERAGE(C2,E2,G2)
3	Male	$S^2=$	0.22	$S^2=$	0.60	$S^2=$	0.38	$N=$	30	=SUM(C4,E4,G4)
4		$N=$	10	$N=$	10	$N=$	10			
5		$M=$	6.75	$M=$	7.95	$M=$	7.49	$M_{female}=$	7.40	=AVERAGE(C5,E5,G5)
6	Female	$S^2=$	0.38	$S^2=$	0.47	$S^2=$	0.32	$N=$	30	=SUM(C7,E7,G7)
7		$N=$	10	$N=$	10	$N=$	10			
9		$M_{control}=$	6.78	$M_{online}=$	7.53	$M_{in\text{-}person}=$	7.50			
10			=AVERAGE(C2,C5)		=AVERAGE(E2,E5)		=AVERAGE(G2,G5)			
11		$N=$	20		20		20			
12			=SUM(C4,C7)		=SUM(E4,E7)		=SUM(G4,G7)			
14	k_{gender}	2	df between for gender		1	=B14-1				
15	$k_{training}$	3	df between for training		2	=B15-1				
16	k_{total}	6	df within for condition		54	=(SUM(C4,C7,E4,E7,G4,G7))-B16				
17			df interaction		2	=(B14-1)*(B15-1)				

	A	B	C
21	Grand mean =	7.27	=AVERAGE(C2,C5,E2,E5,G2,G5)
22	MS Within =	0.40	=(SUM(C3,C6,E3,E6,G3,G6))/B16
23			
24	MS Between training =	3.63	=((C11*(C9-B21)^2)+(E11*(E9-B21)^2)+(G11*(G9-B21)^2))/(B15-1)
25	F for training =	9.20	=B24/B22
26	Probability of F =	0.000	=F.DIST.RT(B25,E15,E16)
27			
28	MS Between gender=	1.01	=((I3*(I2-B21)^2)+(I6*(I5-B21)^2))/(B14-1)
29	F for gender =	2.57	=B28/B22
30	Probability of F =	0.115	=F.DIST.RT(B29,E14,E16)
31			
32			
33	MS between interaction =	1.26	=(((C4*(C2-B21)^2)+(E4*(E2-B21)^2)+(G4*(G2-B21)^2)+(C7*(C5-B21)^2)+(E7*(E5-B21)^2)+(G7*(G5-B21)^2))-((C11*(C9-B21)^2)+(E11*(E9-B21)^2)+(G11*(G9-B21)^2))-(((I3*(I2-B21)^2)+(I6*(I5-B21)^2)))/((B15-1)*(B14-1))
34	F for interaction =	3.20	=B33/B22
35	Probability of F =	0.049	=F.DIST.RT(B34,E17,E16)

	A	B	C
44	$q=$	3.41	
45	HSD =	0.48	=B44*(SQRT(B22/(E4+G4)))
46			
47	$M_{in\text{-}person} - M_{online} =$	0.03	=ABS(G9-E9)
48	$M_{in\text{-}person} - M_{control} =$	0.72	=ABS(G9-C9)
49	$M_{online} - M_{control} =$	0.76	=ABS(E9-C9)
50			

Step 5: Determine k_A. Next, one determines the number of groups, which is k_A. In this example, $k_A = 3$.

Step 6: Calculate $MS_{between\ for\ A}$. Using Eq. 4.20, $MS_{between\ for\ A}$ is computed. This is done in Excel by manually computing the formula given in Eq. 4.20:

$$MS_{between\ for\ A} = \frac{20*(6.78-7.27)^2 + 20*(7.53-7.27)^2 + 20*(7.50-7.27)^2}{2} = 3.63$$

Step 7: Calculate s^2 for each group. In this example, we will not need to calculate these because they are given: 0.22, 0.60, 0.38, 0.38, 0.47 and 0.32. These were calculated using Eq. 4.3 or can be calculated in Excel using the 'var.s' function: = var.s (control, men); = var.s (online, men); = var.s (in-person, men); = var.s (control, women); = var.s (online, women); = var.s (in-person, women).

(Continued)

(Continued)

Step 8: Calculate MS_{within}. Using Eq. 4.25, $MS_{within\ for\ A}$ is computed. This is done in Excel by manually computing the formula given in Eq. 4.25:

$$MS_{within} = \frac{2.37}{6} = 0.40$$

Step 9: Calculate F_A. Using Eq. 4.19, F_A is computed. This is done in Excel by manually computing the formula given in Eq. 4.19:

$$F_A = \frac{3.63}{.40} = 9.20$$

Step 10: Determine the probability associated with $F_{A\ obtained}$. The probability associated with the $F = 9.20$ is < 0.001. This can be determined using the exact probability in a statistics program or using the critical value of 3.17 which is the F-value associated with 2, 54 df and a probability of 0.05. This is done in Excel by using the 'f.dist. rt' function: = f.dist.rt(F-value, df between, df within).

Step 11: Make a decision to reject or fail to reject the null hypothesis. In this case, one rejects the null hypothesis. There is at least one difference among the groups.

Step 12: In cases where the null hypothesis is rejected, decide which post hoc test to use. For this example, we show the results of Tukey's HSD test.

Step 13: If using Tukey's HSD, locate q. One can find the value of q using a q-critical table found in most statistics textbooks and on the internet. Based on k of 3, df_{within} of 57 (60 − 3), and an alpha of 0.05, q is 3.41.

Step 14: Calculate Tukey's HSD. Using Eq. 4.26, Tukey's HSD is computed. This is done in Excel by manually computing the formula given in Eq. 4.26:

$$HSD = 3.41 * \sqrt{\frac{.40}{20}} = 0.48$$

Step 15: Compare the HSD value to the absolute value of the mean difference between each group. Next, each possible comparison is made. These formulas must be manually entered into Excel using subtraction and absolute value ('abs') functions = abs (mean of in person − mean of online), etc.:

$$M_{in\ person} - M_{online} = 7.50 - 7.53 = 0.03$$

|0.03| < 0.48 therefore these two groups are not statistically significantly different from each other.

$$M_{in\ person} - M_{control} = 7.50 - 6.78 = 0.72$$

|0.72| > 0.48 therefore these two groups are statistically significantly different from each other.

$$M_{online} - M_{control} = 7.53 - 6.78 = 0.76$$

|0.98| > 0.48 therefore these two groups are statistically significantly different from each other.

Step 16: Interpret the results in light of the null hypothesis for independent variable A. Participants in the in-person training condition and participants in the online training had statistically significantly higher customer service scores than participants in the control group; however, the scores between the online training and in-person training were not significantly different from each other. The organization should consider implementing the in-person training or the online training, as both types of training significantly increased customer service scores as compared to a group that did not receive training. Given costs, the online training may be a preferable option.

Step 17: State the null hypothesis for the main effect of independent variable B (gender). The null hypothesis is that there are no statistically significant differences in customer service scores in the population of men and women:

$$H_o : \mu_{males} = \mu_{females}$$

Step 18a: Determine $n_{I \text{ of } B}$. This refers to the number of participants exposed to each condition of B (gender). Said otherwise, how many participants in the study are male and how many are female?

Step 18b: Calculate $M_{I \text{ for } B}$. This refers to the mean for each gender. It is computed using Eq. 4.2. Because we are only given the means for each condition by gender, we must collapse across the three training conditions to find the overall mean for males and females. Because the sample sizes are the same, this can be obtained by calculating a simple mean of the means. In the cases of unequal means, a weighted mean is necessary. The same Excel steps listed in step 3 can be used for the process of testing the main effects for variable B:

$$M_{males} = \frac{6.80 + 7.11 + 7.50}{3} = 7.14$$

$$M_{females} = \frac{6.75 + 7.95 + 7.49}{3} = 7.40$$

Step 18c: Calculate M_G. This was previously calculated in testing the main effect of training in step 4. The value is 7.27.

(Continued)

(Continued)

Step 18d: Determine k_B. Next, one determines the number of groups which is k_B. In this example, $k_B = 2$.

Step 18e: Calculate $MS_{between\ for\ B}$. Using Eq. 4.22, $MS_{between\ for\ B}$ is computed:

$$MS_{between\ for\ B} = \frac{30*(7.14-7.27)^2 + 30*(7.40-7.27)^2}{1} = 1.01$$

Step 18f: Calculate MS_{within}. From step 8, MS_{within} is .40 from Eq. 4.25.

Step 18g: Calculate F_B. Using Eq. 4.21, F_B is computed:

$$F_B = \frac{MS_{between\ for\ B}}{MS_{within}} = \frac{1.01}{.40} = 2.57$$

Step 18h: Determine the probability associated with $F_{A\ obtained}$. The probability associated with the $F = 2.57$ is 0.11. This can be determined using the exact probability in a statistics program or using the critical value of 4.02 which is the F-value associated with 1, 54 df and a probability of 0.05.

Step 18i: Make a decision to reject or fail to reject the null hypothesis. In this case, one fails to reject the null hypothesis. Post hoc tests are unnecessary because we failed to reject the null hypothesis. In this case, because there are only two levels of the independent variable, post hoc tests would not have been necessary even if we did reject the null hypothesis.

Step 18j: Interpret the results. Men and women do not differ significantly on their customer service scores.

Step 19: State the null hypothesis for the interaction effect. There is no interaction between training condition and gender. All of the mean differences in the population between treatment conditions can be explained by the main effects of the two independent variables.

Step 20: Determine n_i. This refers to the number of participants exposed to each condition across the study. This value is 10.

Step 21: Calculate M_i. This refers to the mean for each condition. It is computed using Eq. 4.2. These values are displayed in the Excel screenshot.

Step 22: Refer to M_G, which was previously calculated in step 4. This was previously calculated in testing the main effect of training in step 4. The value is 7.27.

Step 23: Calculate $\Sigma n_i * (M_k - M_G)^2$. Using the values from steps 20 to 22, $\Sigma n_i * (M_k - M_G)^2$ is computed. These can be manually calculated in Excel using the listed formula:

$$\Sigma n_i * (M_i - M_G)^2 = 10*(6.80-7.27)^2 + 10*(7.11-7.27)^2 + 10*(7.50-7.27)^2 +$$
$$10*(6.75-7.27)^2 + 10*(7.95-7.27)^2 + 10*(7.49-7.27)^2$$
$$= 10.81$$

Step 24: Calculate $MS_{Between\ for\ AxB}$. Using Eq. 4.24, $MS_{between\ for\ AxB}$ is computed:

$$MS_{between\ for\ AxB} = \frac{10.81 - 7.26 - 1.01}{2*1} = 1.26$$

The values for $\left(\Sigma n_{i\ of\ A} * (M_{i\ of\ A} - M_G)^2\right) and \left(\Sigma n_{i\ of\ B} * (M_{i\ of\ B} - M_G)^2\right)$ were retrieved from previous calculations (numerator of $MS_{between\ for\ A}$ and $MS_{between\ for\ B}$ calculations in steps 6 and 18e).

Step 25: Refer to MS_{within}, **which was previously calculated in step 8.** MS_{within} is 0.40 as determined previously when calculating the value for the main effect of training in step 8 using Eq. 4.25.

Step 26: Calculate F_{AxB}. Using Eq. 4.23, F_{AxB} is computed:

$$F_{AxB} = \frac{1.26}{.40} = 3.20$$

Step 27: Determine the probability associated with F_{AxB}. The probability associated with the $F = 3.20$ is 0.049. This can be determined using the exact probability in a statistics program or using the critical value of 3.17 which is the F-value associated with df of 2, 54 and a probability of 0.05.

Step 28: Make a decision to reject or fail to reject the null hypothesis. In this case, we reject the null hypothesis.

Step 29: In cases where the null hypothesis is rejected, plot the mean values for each condition on a graph to interpret the nature of the interaction effect. The easiest way to interpret an interaction effect is to plot the values on a multiple bar chart. The dependent variable should be on the y-axis, one of the independent variables should be plotted on the x-axis and the other variable should be plotted as two separate bars. This can easily be done in most spreadsheet programs such as Microsoft Excel.

(Continued)

(Continued)

Notice that the interaction appears to be specifically associated with the online training. Women seemed to benefit more from this training than did men. There are no large gender differences apparent in the other training conditions.

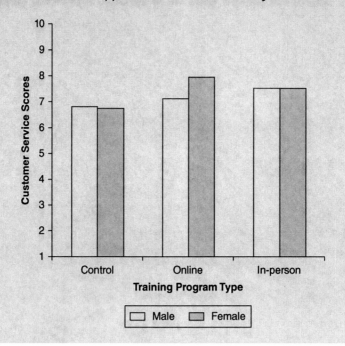

Other complex analysis of variance techniques

In addition to the ANOVA techniques described in this chapter, there are a number of options that can be used depending on the research design and context. These possibilities are briefly reviewed. A two-factor repeated-measures ANOVA is appropriate when two independent variables are involved in a study and both are assessed using a repeated-measures design. Much like the single-factor repeated-measures ANOVA, this test involves a partialling of variance that is attributed to the factors and also allows for the test of an interaction between the two repeated-measures independent variables. A mixed ANOVA should be used in cases where there are two independent variables and one variable is based on a between-subjects design and the other is based on a repeated-measures design.

Furthermore, each of these tests can be extended to incorporate a third independent variable (three-factor ANOVA), such that three main effects, three two-way interactive effects and a three-way interaction can be examined. Analysis of covariance (ANCOVA) is an extension of ANOVA and incorporates some elements of linear

regression (discussed in Part III of this chapter). It statistically controls for varia..
in the dependent variable that is attributable to third variables (called covariates).
Lastly, both ANOVA and ANCOVA have multivariate equivalents, called MANOVA and
MANCOVA, which allow for the evaluation of an independent variable or multiple independent variables on multiple dependent variables.

Part II summary

Two classes of quantitative analyses are commonly used with experimental and
quasi-experimental designs: *t*-tests and ANOVAs. *T*-tests are used when the research
question of interest involves determining whether two samples (which are often
labelled groups or conditions) representing two populations are statistically different
from one another based on a single independent variable. The *t*-test requires that
the data for the dependent variable be on an interval or ratio scale. The *t*-test computation is a ratio of the observed differences between the samples to the expected
differences between the samples. Larger ratios in absolute value terms result in a
greater likelihood of rejecting the null hypothesis or concluding that the two samples,
and therefore populations, are significantly different.

When a research question extends beyond the comparison of two populations
or two independent variables, the class of quantitative analyses known as ANOVA
is appropriate. Like the *t*-test, ANOVA requires that the data for the dependent
variable be on an interval or ratio scale. The calculations for ANOVA involve multiple steps, but the ultimate test statistic (*F*-test) is based on a ratio of the variance
between the multiple samples (each representing a unique population) to the average variance within each sample. Similar to the *t*-test, larger *F*-values result in a
greater likelihood of rejecting the null hypothesis or concluding that the various
samples, and therefore populations, are significantly different. ANOVA can also
be used if a researcher wishes to examine the influence of multiple independent
variables simultaneously on a dependent variable. Using the same logic as above,
the test statistic addresses whether there is a significant difference across various
conditions of each independent variable, as well as whether the two independent
variables significantly interact (i.e. act different in conjunction than in isolation) in
influencing the dependent variable.

PART III: QUANTITATIVE ANALYSES COMMONLY
USED WITH NON-EXPERIMENTAL RESEARCH

When dealing with non-experimental designs, researchers are typically interested in
the degree of relationships between variables rather than comparisons of mean differences. In this part of the chapter, we cover four quantitative analyses that provide

information about the strength and nature of linear relationships between variables, including correlation coefficients, partial correlations, simple ordinary least squares linear regression and multiple ordinary least squares linear regression. The examples presented in this section include the Excel formulas adjacent to the results to display the underlying computations.

Correlation coefficient

In studies where the interest is in determining the relationship between only two variables (often referred to as X and Y), the calculation of a correlation coefficient is appropriate. The precise type of correlation depends on the measurement scale of the variables. All of the types of correlations can use the same null hypothesis, formula and distributions for determining critical values (an alternative computational formula is possible for some types of correlations). The differences lie in the way the data are structured before it is entered in the equations. Table 4.8 outlines the type of correlation used in each situation. It is important to note that correlations can only be used with nominal data when the data are dichotomous, meaning there are only two categories of the variable.

Table 4.8 Type of correlation appropriate according to measurement of the **X** and **Y** variables

		Measurement of Y variable		
		Interval/Ratio	*Ordinal*	*Nominal and dichotomous*
Measurement of X variable	Interval/Ratio	Pearson's product moment correlation		
	Ordinal	Biserial correlation	Spearman's Rho	
	Nominal and dichotomous	Point Biserial	Rank Biserial	Phi Coefficient

Note: X and Y can be used interchangeably. For example, if the X variable is interval/ratio and the Y variable is nominal and dichotomous, a point biserial correlation should be used.

For all types of correlations, the null hypothesis is that there is no relationship between the two variables in the population. P is the symbol used to denote a correlation in the population, while r denotes a correlation in a sample.

$$H_o : P = 0$$

If the analysis is statistically significant, one rejects the null hypothesis and concludes that there is a statistically significant relationship between two variables in the population. Otherwise, one fails to reject the null hypothesis and concludes that there is not enough evidence to suggest a significant correlation between the two variables in the population.

The formula for a correlation is:

$$r_{XY} = \frac{n * \Sigma XY - (\Sigma X) * (\Sigma Y)}{(\sqrt{n * (\Sigma X^2) - (\Sigma X)^2}) * (\sqrt{n * (\Sigma Y^2) - (\Sigma Y)^2})}$$

Eq. 4.28

where X represents an individual's score on one variable, Y represents an individual's score on the second variable and n is the number of pairs of scores. The degrees of freedom for correlations are n - 2. Conceptually, a correlation indexes the covariation between X and Y divided by their respective standard deviations.

Correlations use the t-distribution to determine the probability associated with the observed test result. To do so, r must be converted to t. This conversion is computed via the following formula:

$$t_{obtained} = r * \sqrt{\frac{n-2}{1-r^2}}$$

Eq. 4.29

A few points about the correlation coefficient and the conceptual background of the formula are worth mentioning. First, a correlation coefficient can only range between -1 and 1. If one calculates r and obtains a value outside of this range, a mistake has been made. This is because the formula standardizes the units of each scale and puts them on a common metric. Second, the sign of the correlation conveys the direction of the relationship. A positive correlation indicates that variables tend to change in the same direction. As one variable increases, the other increases as well. An example of this is the correlation between market share and profitability. A negative correlation indicates that variables tend to change in opposite directions or have an inverse relationship. For example, unemployment rates and consumer confidence are negatively related. As unemployment rates increase, consumer confidence in the economy decreases.

Third, the size of correlation conveys information about how strongly two variables are related. Correlations that are closer to 1 and -1 are stronger than those that are closer to zero. Another way to think about the strength of the relationship is in terms of consistency. When two variables are linearly related, a scatterplot of the data (a graph with a point for each person where their standing on X and Y intersect) would result in a straight line. A correlation of 1.0 (or -1.0) means that all points fall perfectly along the line, and thus knowledge of a person's standing on X also gives perfect knowledge of their standing on Y. As correlation coefficients approach 0, it means that the relationships are less consistent and more error is introduced. Although the points may converge around the line, they do not fall perfectly along it. Knowing X in this case gives us some information about Y, but it is less precise.

Points in this scatterplot may converge around the line, but they do not fall perfectly along it. When the correlation is zero, there is no linear relationship, meaning that a person's standing on *X* provides no reliable information about their standing on *Y*. Figure 4.8 shows scatterplots associated with various correlations.

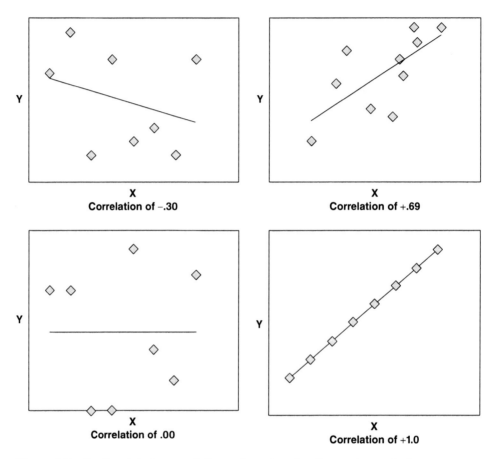

Figure 4.8   Scatterplots for correlations of varying direction and magnitude

The computation for a correlation coefficient involves comparing the degree to which *X* and *Y* vary together to the degree to which each varies independently. The numerator of the equation assesses the covariance by examining the product of the variables minus the product of the individual variables, and the denominator involves calculations of how much deviation occurs within the *X* variable and within the *Y* variable. Larger correlations involve variables that have a large amount of covariance relative to the amount of variance within each variable.

It is important to note that Pearson's product moment correlation is the only correlation that is parametric. The others are non-parametric, meaning they do not require assumptions about the data or the data are not all on an interval or ratio scale. Additionally, most of the correlation coefficients are only suitable to detect linear relationships. Spearman's rho coefficient, which is used when both variables are measured as ordinal variables (e.g. ranks), can detect non-linear relationships. This is because rather than focus on values with inherent meaning or set distances between them, Spearman's rho essentially gives an estimate of how likely a person who ranks first on variable X (or second, third, etc.) is likely to rank first (or second, third, etc.) on variable Y. In a perfectly consistent relationship, the rank order on a person's X variable would perfectly align with that on the Y variable. The steps involved in computing a correlation are summarized in Table 4.9.

Table 4.9 Steps to calculating a correlation

---

1. State the null hypothesis
2. For each participant, multiply X and Y. Sum these values to calculate ΣXY
3. Sum all of the X values to calculate ΣX
4. Sum all of the Y values to calculate ΣY
5. Square each X value, then sum them to get ΣX^2
6. Square each Y value, then sum them to get ΣY^2
7. Calculate r
8. Convert r to $t_{obtained}$
9. Determine the probability associated with $t_{obtained}$
10. Make a decision to reject or fail to reject the null hypothesis
11. Interpret the decision

Box 4.11   Computing a correlation

Bob is a head of finance who does not believe the age-old idiom that happy customers purchase more from a company. To show that he is right, he decides to administer a survey that asks 10 customers about their satisfaction with their experience shopping with the company using a five-point rating scale, where higher values indicate more satisfaction. He then links these data to the number of purchases with the company over the past year. The number of purchases is measured as the number of sales transactions. The data are listed below. Based on these data, is Bob right in his suspicions?

Note that 10 is a small sample size for any research study. We use this small number only for illustration purposes.

(Continued)

(Continued)

Step 1: State the null hypothesis. The null hypothesis is that there is no relationship between customer satisfaction and the number of purchases in the population:

$$H_o : P = 0$$

Recall that although the null hypothesis is focused on the population, we use sample data to test the hypothesis and make inferences about the population.

Steps 2-6: For each participant, multiply X*Y. Sum these values to calculate ΣXY; sum all of the X values to calculate ΣX; sum all of the Y values to calculate ΣY; square each X value, then sum them to get ΣX^2; square each Y value, then sum them to get ΣY^2. These can be calculated by manually setting up formulas in Excel using basic multiplication and exponent functions. Note, however, that if using Excel, this step is not necessary, as one can use the 'correl' function described below with the raw data.

Step 7: Calculate r. Eq. 4.28 is used to calculate r:

$$r = \frac{(10 * 446) - (31 * 133)}{\left(\sqrt{(10 * 109) - 31^2}\right) * \left(\sqrt{(10 * 1975) - 133^2}\right)} = \frac{337}{515.62} = 0.653$$

The correlation analysis can be conducted in Excel using the 'correl' function = correl(customer satisfaction scores for customer ID 1 through 10, number of purchases for customer ID 1 through 10).

	A	B	C	D	E	F	G	H	I	J	K
		Customer Satisfaction		Number of Purchases							
1	Customer ID	(X)		(Y)		X*Y		X^2		Y^2	
2	1	4		17		68	=B2*D2	16	=B2^2	289	=D2^2
3	2	3		15		45	=B3*D3	9	=B3^2	225	=D3^2
4	3	2		12		24	=B4*D4	4	=B4^2	144	=D4^2
5	4	5		19		95	=B5*D5	25	=B5^2	361	=D5^2
6	5	2		13		26	=B6*D6	4	=B6^2	169	=D6^2
7	6	1		5		5	=B7*D7	1	=B7^2	25	=D7^2
8	7	4		19		76	=B8*D8	16	=B8^2	361	=D8^2
9	8	4		8		32	=B9*D9	16	=B9^2	64	=D9^2
10	9	3		9		27	=B10*D10	9	=B10^2	81	=D10^2
11	10	3		16		48	=B11*D11	9	=B11^2	256	=D11^2
12	Sum X =	31	Sum Y =	133	Sum X*Y =	446	Sum X^2 =	109	Sum Y^2 =	1975	
13		=sum(B2:B11)		=sum(D2:D11)		=sum(F2:F11)		=sum(H2:H11)		=sum(J2:J11)	
15	Pearson's r =	0.65		=CORREL(B2:B11,D2:D11)			N =	10			
16	r to t conversion =	2.44		=B15*(SQRT((H16)/(1-B15^2)))			df =	8			
17	Probability of t	0.04		=T.DIST.2T(B16,H16)							

Step 8: Convert r to t$_{obtained}$. Eq. 4.29 is used for this conversion:

$$t_{obtained} = .653 * \sqrt{\frac{8}{.572}} = 2.44$$

Step 9: Determine probability associated with t$_{obtained}$. The probability associated with a $t = |2.44|$ is 0.04. This can be determined using the exact probability in a statistics program or using the critical value of 2.31 which is the t-value associated with 8 df and a probability of 0.05. In Excel, the significance of the correlation can be assessed by converting r to t, using a manually entered formula based on Eq. 4.29. The significance of the t-value can be assessed using the 't.dist.2T' function: = t.dist.2T = (calculated t-value, df).

Step 10: Make a decision to reject or fail to reject the null hypothesis. Based on the size of the correlation and the associated t-value, we reject the null hypothesis.

Step 11: Interpret the decision. The correlation between customer satisfaction and the number of purchases is statistically significantly different from zero. The correlation is positive and fairly large, meaning that as customer satisfaction increases, the number of purchases also tends to increase and vice versa. Bob is wrong – he should believe the old saying!

The previous example (Box 4.11) was a Pearson's product moment correlation because the X and Y variables were measured on interval scales. A similar process is followed for calculating other types of correlations. The only difference is in how the data are structured and special consideration must be given to the interpretation of the correlation coefficient.

Spearman's rho coefficient and biserial correlations

As noted above, the same process is followed to calculate a Spearman's rho coefficient or a biserial correlation, as was followed for Pearson's product moment correlation. The main difference is that the data will be in rank order (both the X and Y variables for Spearman's rho; only one of the variables for biserial). It is important to note that for the ordinal variable(s), the rank ordering must be only within the sample itself. For example, if 10 participants are selected from a population of 100 that is rank ordered, the sample must be reordered so that the ranks range from 1 to 10. In the case of ties, each person should receive the average of the values they would have received had there not been a tie (e.g. two people tied for third place would both be given rank orders of 3.5). Lastly, when interpreting a Spearman's rho or biserial correlation it is important to do so in light of the ordinal nature of the variable. That is, the relationship of interest involves one's rank order on a variable, rather than a person's raw standing. Because the rank orders are sample dependent, these types of correlations can be particularly prone to sample error.

Point biserial, rank biserial and phi coefficient

In the case of these correlation coefficients, at least one of the variables is nominal and dichotomous. When dealing with a nominal dichotomous variable, the researcher must 'dummy code' the variable, which means that an arbitrary numerical code is assigned to each level of the nominal variable. Typically 'O' and '1' are used, but any values can be used. It does not matter what the values are; rather, that the researcher clearly delineates which condition is associated with the higher value. This has implications for how one interprets results. In entering the data, each participant would be assigned a value of either 'O' or '1', depending on their status on the variable in question.

Box 4.12   Computing point-biserial correlations

An operations researcher is interested in the correlation between percentage of customer orders delivered on time and the use of just-in-time manufacturing systems. The use of just-in-time manufacturing systems is a nominal and dichotomous variable and the percentage of customer orders delivered on time is a ratio scale variable. Thus, the appropriate test is the point biserial correlation. If we conduct the analysis and $r = 0.67$, the interpretation of this correlation is entirely dependent on how the use of just-in-time manufacturing systems was coded. If the use of just-in-time manufacturing systems was coded such that 'yes' were given the higher value (e.g. $0 = $ no, $1 = $ yes), then a positive correlation indicates that there is a tendency for the use of just-in-time manufacturing systems to be associated with a higher percentage of customer deliveries being made on time. If the data were

	A	B	C
	On-time Delivery (Y)	Just in Time Manufacturing (X)	
1			
2	70%	0	
3	75%	1	
4	70%	0	
5	60%	0	
6	82%	1	
7	60%	1	
8	55%	0	
9	85%	1	
10	80%	1	
11	57%	0	
12			
13	$r =$	0.67	=CORREL(A2:A11,B2:B11)

coded in the opposite manner, we would conclude that not using these systems is associated with more orders being delivered on time. Moreover, if the correlation were negative (r = -0.67) and the dummy coding was no = 0, yes = 1, then we would conclude that not using these systems is associated with orders being delivered on time, since a negative correlation implies an inverse relationship.

This same idea applies with the rank biserial and the phi coefficient. In the case of the phi coefficient, both variables must be dummy coded; thus, the researcher must pay careful attention to the coding of both variables when interpreting results. Additionally, the phi coefficient (denoted φ) is used in situations where a chi-square test of independence could also be used. The results of each test are directly related, as:

$$\phi = \sqrt{\frac{x^2_{obtained}}{n}}$$

Eq. 4.30

The type of measurement scales involved in a point biserial analysis is also conducive to an independent t-test. These two analyses will give the same answer and t and r can be directly converted to one another using Eq. 4.29.

Partial correlations

Often, researchers are interested in understanding the association between two variables while controlling for the effect of a third variable. This gives a better glimpse of the 'true' relationship between variables. For example, a finding in organizational studies is that employees who experience a high amount of conflict with their supervisors are more likely to commit acts of counterproductive work behaviour (e.g. stealing, cyberloafing at work). However, people who are high in a trait called negative affectivity tend to be more prone to perceiving situations as involving conflict, and they also tend to engage in more counterproductive work behaviour. Thus, the relationship between conflict with supervisor and counterproductive behaviour could be artificially inflated due to the relationship of both variables with negative affectivity. Fortunately, there is a tool that allows researchers to statistically parcel out the effects of a third variable (Z) on the relationship between X and Y. This procedure is called a partial correlation and is best suited for use when all three variables are measured on interval or ratio scales.

Figure 4.9 shows a visual illustration of the example. The area marked 'A' where all three variables overlap represents the amount of variance that is shared by all three variables. The area marked 'B' represents the shared variance between negative affectivity and counterproductive work behaviours, and the area marked 'C' represents the

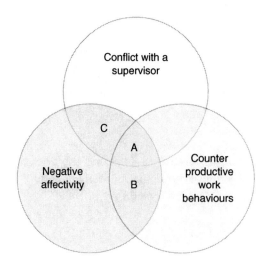

Figure 4.9   Conceptual illustration of partial correlation

shared variance between negative affectivity and conflict with a supervisor. In essence, a partial correlation removes the areas A, B and C from the calculations and gives an estimate of what the correlation between conflict with a supervisor and counterproductive work behaviour would be if negative affectivity could be removed.

The null hypothesis for a partial correlation is that there is no relationship between the two variables X and Y in the population when holding the influence of a third variable, Z, constant. If the analysis is statistically significant, one rejects the null hypothesis and concludes that there is a statistically significant relationship between X and Y in the population, when the effect of Z is held constant. Otherwise, one fails to reject the null hypothesis and concludes that there is not enough evidence to suggest a significant correlation between the two variables in the population when Z is held constant.

The formula for a partial correlation is:

$$r_{XY.Z} = \frac{r_{XY} - (r_{XZ} * r_{YZ})}{\sqrt{(1 - r^2_{XZ}) * (1 - r^2_{YZ})}}$$

Eq. 4.31

where r_{XY} is the correlation between variables X and Y, r_{XZ} is the correlation between variables X and Z, and r_{YZ} is the correlation between variables Y and Z. The degree of freedom for partial correlations is $n - 2$, where n represents the total number of individuals for which all three correlations can be computed. Partial correlations use the t-distribution to determine the probability associated with the observed test result. To do so, r must be converted to t using Eq. 4.29. The steps involved in computing a partial correlation are summarized in Table 4.10.

Table 4.10   Steps to calculating a partial correlation

---

1. State the null hypothesis
2. Calculate r_{XY}, r_{XZ}, and r_{YZ}
3. Calculate $r_{XY.Z}$
4. Convert r to $t_{obtained}$
5. Determine the probability associated with $t_{obtained}$
6. Make a decision to reject or fail to reject the null hypothesis
7. Interpret the decision

Box 4.13   Computing a partial correlation

A researcher is studying the relationship between conflict with a supervisor and counterproductive work behaviours (e.g. theft, wasting resources). She wants to ensure that this relationship is not entirely accounted for by the association of both variables with the personality characteristic negative affectivity. In her sample of 18 employees, the correlation between conflict with a supervisor and counterproductive work behaviours is $r = 0.48$; the correlation between conflict with a supervisor and negative affectivity is $r = 0.33$; and the correlation between negative affectivity and counterproductive work behaviours is $r = 0.28$.

Step 1: State the null hypothesis. There is no relationship between conflict with a supervisor and counterproductive work behaviour in the population when holding the influence of negative affectivity constant. Recall that although the null hypothesis is focused on the population, we use sample data to test the hypothesis and make inferences about the population.

Step 2: Calculate r_{XY}, r_{XZ}, and r_{YZ} . In this example, the values are given to us and can be used to compute the partial correlation. If we were working with raw data, we would use Eq. 4.28 and conduct three separate analyses using the correlation function in Excel to obtain the three correlation coefficients. We can call r_{XY} the correlation between conflict with a supervisor and counterproductive work behaviours, r_{YZ} the correlation between conflict with a supervisor and negative affectivity, and r_{YZ} the correlation between counterproductive work behaviours and negative affectivity.

Step 3: Calculate $r_{XY.Z}$. This is done using Eq. 4.31. This can be done in Excel by manually entering the formula based on Eq. 4.31:

$$r_{XY.Z} = \frac{.48 - (.33 * .28)}{\sqrt{(.893) * (.924)}} = 0.43$$

(Continued)

(Continued)

	A	B	C	D	E	F	G
1	Supervisor Conflict	CWB	Neg Aff				
2	5	4	4		df	16	=count(A2:A19)-2
3	4	4	3		r conflict & CWB	0.48	=correl(A2:A19, B2:B19)
4	3	3	4		r conflict & NA	0.33	=correl(A2:A19, C2:C19)
5	4	5	5		r CWB & NA	0.28	=correl(B2:B19, C2:C19)
6	4	4	4				
7	4	4	3		Partial r =	0.43	=(F3-(F5*F4))/(SQRT((1-F5^2)*(1-F4^2)))
8	5	4	3		t =	1.89	=F7*SQRT((F2/(1-F7^2)))
9	4	4	3		Probability of t	0.08	=T.DIST.2T(F8,F2)
10	4	4	4				
11	4	4	4				
12	3	3	1				
13	3	2	3				
14	5	3	4				
15	5	5	3				
16	5	4	4				
17	3	4	3				
18	4	4	3				
19	4	4	2				

Step 4: Convert r to $t_{obtained}$. This is done using Eq. 4.29. This can be done in Excel by manually entering the formula in Eq. 4.29:

$$t_{obtained} = .43 * \sqrt{\frac{16}{.82}} = 1.89$$

Step 5: Determine the probability associated with $t_{obtained}$. The probability associated with a $t = |1.89|$ is $< .08$. This can be determined using the exact probability in a statistics program or using the critical value of 2.12 which is the t-value associated with 16 df and a probability of 0.05. The significance of the t-value can be assessed using the 't.dist.2T' function: $=$ t.dist.2T $=$ (calculated t-value, df).

Step 6: Make a decision to reject or fail to reject the null hypothesis. Based on the size of the correlation and the associated t-value, we fail to reject the null hypothesis.

Step 7: Interpret the decision. The correlation between conflict with supervisor and counterproductive work behaviours is not statistically significantly different from zero, when holding the influence of negative affectivity constant. Notice that the correlation decreased from 0.48 to 0.43, once negative affectivity was partialled out. In the process, the relationship decreases enough so that it is no longer statistically significant, indicating that conflict with a supervisor is associated with counterproductive work behaviours largely as a result of negative affectivity.

Simple ordinary least squares linear regression

Correlations allow one to understand the relationship between two variables or how closely they conform to a line of best fit. This relationship is conceptually explained in the context of prediction (i.e. if we know one's standing on X, how accurately can we predict their standing on Y?), but a correlation does not allow for actual prediction. However, simple ordinary least squares linear regression does. Through the process of linear regression, a linear equation in the form of $\hat{Y} = b_0 + b_1X$ is produced, where $\hat{Y}$ is the predicted score based on a known value of X, b_1 is the slope of the line and b_0 is the intercept of the line, which is determined based on calculations that estimate a line of best fit for the data (see Figure 4.10). The intercept represents the point where the line crosses the y-axis on a scatterplot. The slope indicates the amount of change in Y for a one unit change in X.

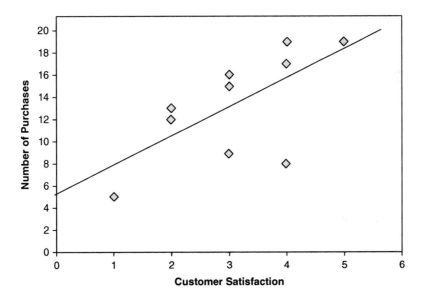

Figure 4.10   Illustration of simple linear regression

The line of best fit produces the smallest squared difference on average between the predicted values of Y and the actual values of Y. Hence, we use the term least squares. The significance of the predictive equation is determined by examining whether b_1 is significantly different from zero. Simple linear regression requires that the Y variable (often labelled the criterion) be measured on an interval or ratio scale. Other forms of regression can be used when the criterion is nominal (logistic regression) or ordinal (ordinal logistic regression). The X variable (often labelled the predictor) can be a nominal and dichotomous variable, an interval or a ratio variable.

The null hypothesis is that the slope of the line of best fit is equal to zero, which also implies that the variance accounted for in the criterion variable by the regression equation is equal to zero in the population. If the analysis is statistically significant, one rejects the null hypothesis and concludes that the slope of the line of best fit is significantly different from zero and that the regression equation accounts for an amount of variance that is significantly greater than zero. Otherwise, one fails to reject the null hypothesis and concludes that there is not enough evidence to suggest that the slope of the line of best fit is significantly different from zero and that the regression equation accounts for an amount of variance that is significantly greater than zero.

Additionally, one can test the statistical significance of the regression coefficients for individual predictors. In these cases, one tests the null hypothesis that a value of a coefficient for a predictor equals zero. If the analysis is statistically significant, one rejects the null hypothesis and concludes that the value of the coefficient is significantly different from zero. Otherwise, one fails to reject the null hypothesis and concludes that there is not enough evidence to suggest that the value of the coefficient is significantly different from zero.

The formula for the coefficients of the simple ordinary least squares linear regression equation is:

$$b_1 = \frac{(n * \Sigma XY) - (\Sigma X * \Sigma Y)}{(n * \Sigma X^2) - (\Sigma x)^2} \qquad \text{Eq. 4.32}$$

$$b_0 = M_y - (b_1 * M_x) \qquad \text{Eq. 4.33}$$

where X represents an individual's score on the predictor variable, Y represents an individual's score on the criterion variable, n is the number of pairs of scores, M_y is the mean for the scores on variable Y and M_x is the mean for the scores on variable X. There are two degrees of freedom for linear regression, calculated as k and $n-k-1$, where k is number of predictors, which in simple ordinary least squares regression is always 1, and n is the sample size.

Simple ordinary least squares linear regression uses the F-distribution to determine the probability associated with the observed test result. To do so, r must be converted to F, using Eq. 4.34:

$$F_{obtained} = \frac{r^2 * (n - k - 1)}{k * (1 - r^2)} \qquad \text{Eq. 4.34}$$

where r is the correlation between X and Y and k is the number of predictors, which in simple ordinary least squares linear regression is always 1, and n is the sample size.

Notice that the calculation of the slope b_1 is somewhat similar to that of the calculation of the correlation. In fact, when b_1 is standardized (which is achieved by converting the X and Y variables to z-scores before analyses using Eq. 4.1), it is identical to r. Further, the significance of the entire equation is driven largely by r (r^2), as it is used to compute $F_{obtained}$. The equation for the F-ratio likely does not appear familiar, but it actually represents a ratio of the variance associated with the regression equation to the variance associated with error.

To test the statistical significance of the individual predictors, one divides the value of the regression coefficient by its standard error. This ratio forms a t-test. The value of this test can be compared to a t-distribution to determine the probability associated with the observed test result.

Table 4.11   Steps to calculating a simple ordinary least squares regression

1. State the null hypothesis
2. Sum all of the X values to calculate ΣX
3. Sum all of the Y values to calculate ΣY
4. Square each X value, then sum them to get ΣX^2
5. Multiply each X and Y, then sum them to get ΣXY
6. Calculate b_1
7. Calculate M_y and M_x
8. Calculate b_0
9. Create an equation in the form of $\hat{Y} = b_0 + b_1 X$
10. Compute r_{XY}
11. Calculate $F_{obtained}$
12. Determine the probability associated with $F_{obtained}$
13. Make a decision to reject or fail to reject the null hypothesis
14. Interpret the decision and, if desired, make predictions based on the equation

Box 4.14   Conducting simple linear regression

Using the same data from the correlation example in Box 4.11, one can calculate a regression equation so that a customer's actual purchases can be predicted from their level of satisfaction. Also, one can determine if this equation is significant. Recall that the data are from 10 customers who completed a survey about their satisfaction using a five-point rating scale, where higher values indicate more satisfaction and their actual purchase behaviour. Note that 10 is a small sample size for any research study. We use this small number only for illustration purposes.

Step 1: State the null hypothesis. The slope of the line of best fit is equal to zero and the variance accounted for in purchases by the regression equation is equal to

(Continued)

(Continued)

zero in the population. Recall that although the null hypothesis is focused on the population, we use sample data to test the hypothesis and make inferences about the population.

	A	B	C	D	E	F
1	Customer ID	Customer Satisfaction	Number of Purchases	Squared Customer Satisfaction	Squared Number of Purchases	Customer Satisfaction * Number of Purchases
2	1	4	17	16	289	68
3	2	3	15	9	225	45
4	3	2	12	4	144	24
5	4	5	19	25	361	95
6	5	2	13	4	169	26
7	6	1	5	1	25	5
8	7	4	19	16	361	76
9	8	4	8	16	64	32
10	9	3	9	9	81	27
11	10	3	16	9	256	48
12	**Sums**	31	133	109	1975	446

	A	B	C	D	E	F
18	b_1	b_0	2.61	5.20	N =	10
19	Standard Error for b_1	Standard Error for b_0	1.07	3.53	df =	8
20	R^2	Standard Error of the	0.43	3.84	k =	1
21	F	df	5.97	8	=LINEST(C2:C11, B2:B11. TRUE, TRUE)	
22						
23	Probability of F	0.04	=F.DIST.RT(C21,F20,F19)			
24	*t*-test for *b1*	2.44	=C18/C19			
25	Probability of *t*	0.04	=T.DIST.2T(B24,F19)			

Steps 2–5: Calculate ΣXY, ΣX, ΣY, ΣX^2. These values are calculated in Excel in the row labelled sums.

Step 6: Calculate b_1. This is calculated using Eq. 4.32:

$$b_1 = \frac{(10*446)-(31*133)}{(10*109)-(31)^2} = 2.61$$

In Excel, these values can be computed using the 'linest' function: =linest(number of purchases for customer ID 1 through 10, customer satisfaction scores for customer ID 1 through 10, TRUE, TRUE). An array must then be created using the CTRL + SHFT + ENTER function and highlighting the cells in two adjacent columns and four rows. This produces b_0 and b_1.

Step 7: Calculate M_y and M_x. These are calculated using Eq. 4.2 and the 'average' function in Excel:

$$M_y = \frac{133}{10} = 13.3$$

$$M_x = \frac{31}{10} = 3.1$$

Step 8: Calculate b_0. This is calculated using Eq. 4.33 and through the 'linest' function:

$$b_0 = 13.3 - (2.61 * 3.1) = 5.20$$

Step 9: Create an equation in the form of $\hat{Y} = b_0 + b_1X$:

$$\hat{Y} = 5.20 + 2.61X$$

Step 10: Compute r_{xy}. This is calculated using Eq. 4.28. We have already calculated this in the context of the previous example for computing a correlation, $r = 0.653$.

Step 11: Calculate $F_{obtained}$. This is calculated using Eq. 4.34 and as part of the 'linest' function:

$$F_{obtained} = \frac{.653^2 * (10 - 1 - 1)}{1 * (1 - .653^2)} = 5.97$$

Step 12: Determine the probability associated with $F_{obtained}$. The probability associated with an $F = 5.97$ is 0.04. This can be determined using the exact probability in a statistics program or using the critical value of 5.32, which is the F-value associated with 1, 8 df and a probability of 0.05. In Excel, the significance of the regression equation can be assessed by calculating F, using a manually entered formula based on Eq. 4.34. The significance of the F-value can be assessed using the 'f.dist.rt' function = f.dist.rt = (calculated F-value, k, df).

Step 13: Make a decision to reject or fail to reject the null hypothesis. Based on the size of $F_{obtained}$, we reject the null hypothesis. Additionally, a test of individual predictors can be executed by dividing the value for b_1 by its standard error. This ratio forms a t-test. The statistical significance of the t can be evaluated using a t-distribution using the t-distribution function in Excel: =T.DIST.2T(t-value, df). In this case, the value of b_1 is statistically significant as the probability is less than 0.05.

Step 14: Interpret the decision and, if desired, make predictions based on the equation. The regression equation is statistically significant, meaning we can predict a customer's purchases if we know their level of satisfaction, using the equation $\hat{Y} = 5.20 + 2.61X$. A customer with a satisfaction score of 3 would be expected to make 13.03 purchases.

Multiple ordinary least squares linear regression

Multiple ordinary least squares linear regression is an extension of simple ordinary least squares linear regression. Instead of creating a predictive equation based only on a single predictor (X) variable, multiple ordinary least squares linear regression allows one to form an equation that incorporates multiple predictors in relation to a single criterion (Y) variable. This type of regression is very common in business and management research.

Multiple ordinary least squares linear regression produces the following equation: $\hat{Y} = b_0 + b_1X_1 + b_2X_2 + b_3X_3 \ldots + b_kX_k$ where each X represents a unique predictor variable, b_0 represents the intercept and each b represents the slope associated with each predictor variable, which is based on the line of best fit using the method of ordinary least squares fitting process that was previously described. Similar to simple linear regression, multiple linear regression requires that the criterion variable be measured on an interval or ratio scale. Predictor variables can be nominal and dichotomous, interval or ratio. Steps can also be taken using advanced dummy coding with predictors that are nominal with more than two levels.

Beyond allowing a researcher to examine multiple variables simultaneously, multiple linear regression is particularly useful because it allows one to examine the unique effects of each X variable, taking into account the effects of all the other X variables on Y. In other words, similar to what we discussed with a partial correlation, regression analyses hold constant the effect of all other variables. This allows one to see the unique variance associated with each predictor variable. Such information is useful in decision-making contexts. For example, if multiple pieces of information are used for making insurance decisions and there is substantial overlap between them (e.g. number of auto accidents and typical driving speed), such that only one is uniquely predicting insurance losses when the effects of the other are held constant, this is a signal that time and money can be saved by using only one of the predictors.

The calculations involved in multiple ordinary least squares linear regression become very complicated when there are more than two predictors in the model. The calculations rely on matrix algebra. To give the reader a general sense of the process involved in multiple linear regression, we provide an example with only two predictors. In cases of more than two predictors, statistical software programs should be used.

The formula for the coefficients of multiple ordinary least squares linear regression equation is:

$$b_1 = \frac{r_{YX_1} - (r_{YX_2} * r_{X_1X_2})}{1 - (r_{X_1X_2})^2} * \frac{s_y}{s_{x_1}}$$

Eq. 4.35

$$b_2 = \frac{r_{YX_2} - (r_{YX_1}) * (r_{X_1X_2})}{1 - (r_{X_1X_2})^2} * \frac{s_y}{s_{x_2}}$$

Eq. 4.36

$$b_0 = M_y - (b_1 * M_{x1}) - (b_2 * M_{x2})$$

Eq. 4.37

where r_{YX_1} represents the correlation between predictor variable X_1 and criterion Y, r_{YX_2} represents the correlation between predictor variable X_2 and criterion Y, $r_{X_1X_2}$ represents the correlation between predictor variable X_1 and predictor variable X_2, S_y is the standard deviation of criterion Y, S_{X_1} is the standard deviation of predictor X_1, S_{X_2} is the standard deviation of predictor X_2, M_y is the mean for the scores on criterion Y, M_{X_1} is the mean for the scores on variable X_1 and M_{X_2} is the mean for the scores on variable X_2. There are two different degrees of freedom for linear regression, calculated as k and $n-k-1$, where k is the number of predictors and n is the total number of participants.

Multiple linear regression uses the F-distribution to determine the probability associated with the observed test result. To do so, r must be converted to F using Eq. 4.34. Because there are multiple correlations factored into r^2, it must be calculated using the following equation (and is labelled with a capital R to denote the multiple correlations):

$$R^2 = \frac{(r_{YX_1})^2 + (r_{YX_2})^2 - 2*(r_{YX_1}*r_{YX_2}*r_{X_1X_2})}{1-(r_{X_1X_2})^2}$$

Eq. 4.38

Notice that the equations are an extension of those used in simple linear regression but take into account both X variables. The process of calculating $F_{obtained}$ is also similar, except the R^2 value now cannot be calculated as a simple correlation between X and Y and must take into account all combinations of correlations between the three variables. The R is capitalized in cases where it is not a simple correlation between two variables, hence the change in notation from the simple linear regression example. In these cases, it is called the multiple correlation. Note that the F-value indicates the significance of the overall regression equation for predicting an outcome, but not the individual predictors. The significance of each b can also be evaluated, based on calculation of a t-statistic. To compute the t-statistic, one divides the value of the regression coefficient by its standard error. The value of this test can be compared to a t-distribution to determine the probability associated with the observed test result.

The formulas above give estimates of the slope terms in a non-standardized form. This means that each is specific to the metric of the variable associated with it. When slopes are in non-standardized form, one cannot simply compare two slopes to make inferences about which is larger. In order to do this, they must be standardized, which can be done by removing $\frac{S_y}{S_{X_2}}$ or $\frac{S_y}{S_{X_1}}$ from the b equation. The benefit to standardization is that it allows one to directly compare slopes, which in standardized form are called betas. It also simplifies the formula, removing the intercept, which will always be zero because the standardization process makes it so the mean of each variable is zero. The drawback to using betas is that any raw data that are entered into the equation for prediction purposes must also be standardized using Eq. 4.1.

Table 4.12   Steps to calculating a multiple ordinary least squares regression with two predictors

---

1. State the null hypothesis
2. Calculate r_{YX_1}, r_{YX_2}, $r_{X_1X_2}$,
3. Calculate S_{X_1}, S_{X_2}, S_Y
4. Calculate b_1 and b_2
5. Calculate M_y and M_x
6. Calculate b_0
7. Create an equation in the form of $\hat{y} = b_0 + b_1X_1 + b_2X_2$
8. Compute R^2
9. Calculate $F_{obtained}$
10. Determine the probability associated with $F_{obtained}$
11. Make a decision to reject or fail to reject the null hypothesis
12. Interpret the decision and, if desired, make predictions based on the equation

---

Box 4.15   Conducting multiple regression

FixIt Corporation is interested in redesigning its employee hiring practices for equipment mechanics. It wants to be sure that the assessments being used during the applicant screening process predict job performance. The company wants to create an equation that allows it to enter an applicant's score on a mechanical aptitude test and on a conscientiousness personality inventory to predict eventual job performance. In undergoing this process, current employees are used to obtain the data, which means administering the new assessment to the 19 current employees and evaluating the scores in relation to the employees' job performance. Job performance is measured on a 1–5 scale, mechanical aptitude is measured on a 30–60 scale and conscientiousness is measured on a scale that ranges from 10 to 40. In all cases, higher values indicate more positive scores (i.e. better job performance, more aptitude, etc.).

Step 1: State the null hypothesis. The variance accounted for in job performance by mechanical aptitude and conscientiousness is equal to zero in the population. Recall that although the null hypothesis is focused on the population, we use sample data to test the hypothesis and make inferences about the population.

Step 2: Calculate r_{YX_1}, r_{YX_2}, $r_{X_1X_2}$. We can calculate each value using Eq. 4.28 and the correlation function in Excel.

Step 3: Calculate S_{x_1}, S_{x_2}, S_Y. We can calculate each value using Eq. 4.3 and using the 'stdev.s' function in Excel.

Step 4: Calculate b_1 and b_2. These are calculated using Eqs 4.35 and 4.36, respectively:

$$b_1 = \frac{.62 - (.89*.55)}{1 - .55^2} * \frac{0.88}{6.91} = 0.02$$

$$b_2 = \frac{.89 - (.62*.55)}{1 - .55^2} * \frac{0.88}{8.38} = 0.08$$

In Excel, these values can be computed using the 'linest' function =linest(job performance values, mechanical aptitude and conscientiousness values, TRUE, TRUE). An array must then be created using the CTRL + SHFT + ENTER function and

	A	B	C	D
1		Job Performance (Y)	Mechanical Aptitude (X_1)	Conscientiousness (X_2)
2		5	59	37
3		4	50	30
4		2	42	12
5		4	48	18
6		4	46	38
7		4	38	31
8		5	55	36
9		3	39	22
10		4	49	28
11		4	49	31
12		3	42	19
13		3	41	16
14		5	58	39
15		5	50	40
16		5	49	33
17		3	41	21
18		4	32	28
19		4	47	30
20		3	50	22
21	Mean	3.89	46.58	27.95
22	Standard Deviation	0.88	6.91	8.38

	K	L	M	N	O	P	Q	R	S	T
1	b_2	b_1	b_0	0.082	0.024	0.506	=LINEST(B2:B20,C2:D20, TRUE, TRUE)			
2	Standard Error for b_2	Standard Error for b_1	Standard Error for b_0	0.014	0.017	0.653				
3		R^2	Standard Error of the Estimate	0.809	0.406					
4		F	df	33.862	16					
5										
6		Probability of F =	0.000002	=F.DIST.RT(N4,R7,R8)			$n =$	19		
7							$k =$	2		
8		$r_{zx_1} =$	0.62	=CORREL(B2:B20,C2:C20)			$df2$	16	=R6-R7-1	
9		$r_{zx_2} =$	0.89	=CORREL(B2:B20,D2:D20)						
10		$r_{x_1 x_2} =$	0.55	=CORREL(C2:C20,D2:D20)						
11										
12		t-test for b_1 =	1.426	=O1/O2						
13		Probability of t =	0.173	=T.DIST.2T(M12,R8)						
14										
15		t-test for b_2 =	5.986	=N1/N2						
16		Probability of t =	0.00002	=T.DIST.2T(M15,R8)						

(Continued)

(Continued)

highlighting the cells in three adjacent columns and four rows. It is important to note that the output of the 'linest' function will provide the value for b_2 first.

Step 5: Calculate M_y and M_x. We can calculate each value using Eq. 4.2 and the 'average' function in Excel.

Step 6: Calculate b_0. This is calculated using Eq. 4.37. The intercept is computed as part of the 'linest' function which is part of step 4:

$$b_0 = 3.89 - .02*46.58 - .08*27.95 = 0.51$$

Step 7: Create an equation in the form of $\hat{Y} = b_0 + b_1X_1 + b_2X_2$:

$$\hat{Y} = 0.51 + 0.02X_1 + 0.08X_2$$

Step 8: ComputerR^2. This is calculated using Eq. 4.38 and as part of the 'linest' function:

$$R^2 = \frac{.62^2 + .89^2 - 2*(.62*.89*.55)}{1 - (.55)^2} = 0.81$$

Step 9: Compute $F_{obtained}$. This is calculated using Eq. 4.34 and as part of the 'linest' function:

$$F_{obtained} = \frac{.81*(19 - 2 - 1)}{2*(.81)} = 33.86$$

Step 10: Determine the probability associated with $F_{obtained}$. The probability associated with an $F = 33.86$ is < 0.001. This can be determined using the exact probability in a statistics program or using the critical value of 3.63, which is the F-value associated with 2, 16 df and a probability of 0.05. In Excel, the significance of the regression equation can be assessed by using the 'f.dist.rt' function = f.dist. rt = (calculated F-value, k, df).

Step 11: Make a decision to reject or fail to reject the null hypothesis. Based on the $F_{obtained}$, we reject the null hypothesis. Additionally, a test of individual predictors can be executed by dividing the value for b_1 by its standard error and b_2 by its standard error. This ratio forms a t-test. The statistical significance of the t can be evaluated using a t-distribution using the t-distribution function in Excel: =T.DIST.2T(t-value, df). In this case, the value of b_1 is not statistically significant as the probability is greater than 0.05. However, the value of b_2 is statistically significant as the probability is less than 0.05.

Step 12: Interpret the decision and, if desired, make predictions based on the equation. The regression equation is statistically significant, meaning we can predict someone's job performance reliably if we know their score on the mechanical aptitude test and conscientiousness inventory, using the equation $\hat{Y} = 0.51 + 0.02X_1 + 0.08X_2$. A person with a mechanical aptitude score of 55 and conscientiousness score of 32 would be expected to have a job performance rating of 4.17.

Part III summary

As described in Part III, there are numerous quantitative analyses that can be used when the question of interest is the relationship between variables, a question that is common in non-experimental research. The most basic test of relationships is a correlation, with the type of correlation (Pearson's product moment, biserial, point biserial, Spearman's rho, phi coefficient) depending on the scale of numerical measurement of the variables. Simple linear regression is an extension of the correlation, and it allows researchers to produce an equation that is useful for predicting actual criterion values (Y) based on the value of the predictor variables (X). Oftentimes, researchers are interested in the relationship between two variables controlling for the effects of a third variable. Partial correlations and multiple linear regression can be used for this purpose, with the difference between the two analyses lying in the equation-generating ability of regression analyses. Mathematically speaking, at the heart of each of these analyses is the comparison of a ratio of the covariance between variables to the variance of each variable alone. Lastly, although correlation and regression analyses are useful and quite common in business and management studies, users of these methods must be careful not to draw causal inferences when not merited by the study design. Causal conclusions can only be drawn from experimental research studies.

PART IV: QUANTITATIVE ANALYSIS COMMONLY USED WHEN DISTRIBUTIONAL ASSUMPTIONS ARE VIOLATED

As mentioned at the beginning of the chapter, non-parametric tests (sometimes called distribution-free tests) do not require the same assumptions about a population distribution as do parametric tests. When the dependent variable is ordinal or nominal data, assumptions about the distribution cannot be made, so non-parametric tests must be used. Sometimes even when data are measured on an interval or ratio scale, the assumptions are not met and non-parametric tests should be used. For most study designs, there are multiple parametric and non-parametric alternatives to test hypotheses. In this part of the chapter, we review two common non-parametric quantitative analyses in detail - the Mann-Whitney U test and the chi-square test of independence, and summarize many of the other options that are available (see Gibbons, 1993 or Siegel and Castellan, 1998 for reviews of these other tests).

The Mann-Whitney U test

When the design of the study is between-subjects, only two conditions or levels of the independent variable are being compared and the dependent variable is measured using an ordinal measurement scale, the Mann-Whitney U test is appropriate. Because this is a non-parametric test, it is less powerful than the parametric equivalent (independent t-test). This test examines differences in medians and ranks of the data instead of the means.

For this analysis, the null hypothesis is that there is an equal likelihood that the rank of an observation selected from condition 1 exceeds the rank of an observation selected from condition 2, or vice versa. If the result of the analysis is statistically significant, one rejects the null hypothesis and concludes that there is a significantly different likelihood that the rank of an observation selected from condition 1 exceeds the rank of an observation selected from condition 2, or vice versa. Otherwise, one fails to reject the null hypothesis and concludes that there is not enough evidence to suggest that there is a significantly different likelihood that the rank of an observation selected from condition 1 exceeds the rank of an observation selected from condition 2, or vice versa.

The formula for the Mann-Whitney U test is:

$$U = n_1 * n_2 + \frac{NX * (NX + 1)}{2} - TX$$

Eq. 4.39

where n_1 is the size of the sample in condition 1, n_2 is the size of the sample in condition 2, NX is the number of people in the group that gave the smaller rank total and TX is the value of the smaller of the two summed ranks.

With sample sizes larger than 30, the Mann-Whitney U test uses the z-distribution to make decisions about probability. The U must be converted into a z-score as follows:

$$z = \frac{U - M_u}{\sigma_m}$$

Eq. 4.40

$$M_u = \frac{n_1 * n_2}{2}$$

Eq. 4.41

$$\sigma_m = \sqrt{\frac{n_1 * n_2 * (n_1 + n_2 + 1)}{12}}$$

Eq. 4.42

The steps involved in computing a Mann-Whitney U test are summarized in Table 4.13.

Table 4.13 Steps to calculating a Mann-Whitney U test

1. State the null hypothesis
2. Rank all of the scores across both samples together, with 1 being the highest and ties being given the average of the ranks that would have been obtained had they been different from each other
3. Sum the ranks for condition 1
4. Sum the ranks for condition 2
5. Determine TX from the smaller of the sums in steps 3 and 4
6. Determine NX
7. Compute U
8. Convert U to Z
9. Determine the probability associated with the $Z_{obtained}$
10. Make a decision to reject or fail to reject the null hypothesis
11. Interpret the decision

Box 4.16   Conducting a Mann-Whitney U test

Huge Hit Records wishes to know if there is a difference in the quality of the vendors used by its Marketing versus Accounting departments. Vendors are rated on a 50–100-point scale based on their performance on their service level agreements. Higher scores represent better performance. Capital Records wants this question assessed using the current vendors, which includes 16 vendors for each department. After collecting the data, it realizes that the data are exceptionally skewed. There is a concern that the shape of the data will violate the assumptions of the parametric quantitative analyses that staff intended to conduct. Instead, it is decided that non-parametric analyses would be more appropriate and the company decides to use a Mann-Whitney U to test for differences in the service levels between the two departments.

Step 1: State the null hypothesis. The null hypothesis is that there is an equal likelihood that the rank of a vendor from Marketing exceeds the rank of a vendor from Accounting and that there is an equal likelihood that the rank of a vendor from Accounting exceeds the rank of a vendor from Marketing. Recall that although the null hypothesis is focused on the population, we use sample data to test the hypothesis and make inferences about the population.

Step 2: Rank all of the scores across both samples together. In the ranks, the highest or most positive score should be given the rank of '1'. Notice that ties are given the average of the values that would have been assigned had there not been a tie.

(Continued)

(Continued)

	A	B	C	D	E	F	G	H
1	Marketing		Accounting					
2	Overall Rank	Score	Overall Rank	Score				
3	3.5	97	1.5	99				
4	5.5	96	1.5	99				
5	5.5	96	3.5	97	sum marketing ranks	268.50	=SUM(A3:A18)	
6	7	95	9.5	92	sum accounting ranks	259.50	=SUM(C3:C18)	
7	8	93	11	90	TX =	259.50	=MIN(G5,G6)	
8	9.5	92	12	88				
9	14.5	85	13	87	N for marketing	16	=COUNT(A3:A18)	
10	17	84	14.5	85	N for accounting	16	=COUNT(C3:C18)	
11	17	84	17	84	NX =	16		
12	20	82	19	83				
13	22	81	22	81	U =	132.50	=(G9*G10)+((G11*(G11+1))/2)-G7	
14	24	80	22	81				
15	26	79	26	79	Z =	0.17	=(G13-((G9*G10)/2))/(SQRT(G9*G10*(G9+G10+1)/12))	
16	29	77	26	79	p-value of Z =	0.57	=NORM.S.DIST(G15,TRUE)	
17	29	77	29	77				
18	31	76	32	75				

Step 3: Sum the overall ranks for condition 1 (Marketing group). The sum of the ranks for the Marketing group is 268.50. This step is conducted in Excel using the 'sum' function: =sum(marketing rank 1 to marketing rank 16).

Step 4: Sum the overall ranks for condition 2 (Accounting group). The sum of the ranks for the accounting group was 259.50. This step is conducted in Excel using the 'sum' function: =sum(accounting rank 1 to accounting rank 16).

Step 5: Determine TX. By comparing the values (268.50 > 259.50), the value of TX is set to 259.50. This is done in Excel using the 'min' function = min (the sum for marketing, the sum for accounting).

Step 6: Determine NX. The N of TX (Accounting group) = 16.

Step 7: Calculate U. Using Eq. 4.39, the value of U can be computed. This must be manually computed in Excel:

$$U = 16 * 16 + \frac{16 * (16+1)}{2} - 259.5 = 132.50$$

Step 8: Convert U to Z. The value of M_u is computed from Eq. 4.41:

$$M_u = \frac{16 * 16}{2} = 128.00$$

The value of σ_m is computed from Eq. 4.42:

$$\sigma_m = \sqrt{\frac{16 * 16 * (16 + 16 + 1)}{12}} = 26.53$$

The value of Z is computed from Eq. 4.40:

$$Z = \frac{U - M_u}{\sigma_m} = \frac{132.50 - 128.00}{26.53} = .17$$

Step 9: Determine the probability associated with $Z_{obtained}$. The probability associated with the $Z = |.17|$ is $p = .57$. This can be determined using the exact probability in a statistics program or using the critical value of 1.96 which is the Z-value associated with a probability of 0.05. In Excel, the significance of the test can be assessed by converting U to Z, using a manually entered formula based on Eq. 4.40. The significance of the Z-value can be assessed using the 'normal.s.dist' function = 'normal.s.dist' = (calculated z-value, TRUE).

Step 10: Make a decision to reject or fail to reject the null hypothesis. In this case, one would fail to reject the null hypothesis.

Step 11: Interpret the decision. There are not statistically significant differences in the rank order of vendors based on department.

Chi-square test of independence

When the design of the study is between-subjects, any number of conditions of the independent variable are being compared and the dependent variable is measured using a nominal measurement scale, the chi-square test of independence is appropriate to determine the association between variables. Because this is a non-parametric test, it is less powerful than the parametric equivalent (independent t-test). Note that this test can be used when there are more than two conditions present. The only factor that changes is the number of values that are summed in the calculations.

The null hypothesis of this analysis is that the distribution of the dependent variable is the same across the levels of the independent variable. If the results are statistically significant, one rejects the null hypothesis and concludes that the distribution of the dependent variable is significantly different across the levels of the independent variable. Otherwise, one fails to reject the null hypothesis and concludes that there is not enough evidence to suggest the distribution of the dependent variable is significantly different across the levels of the independent variable. The chi-square test of independence uses the chi-square distribution to determine the probability associated with the observed test result.

The formula for a chi-square test of independence is:

$$X^2_{obtained} = \Sigma \frac{(f_o - f_e)^2}{f_e} \qquad \text{Eq. 4.43}$$

$$f_e \, for \, condition_{iVlevel i, DVlevel j} = \frac{f_o \, for \, IV_{level i} \, * f_o \, for \, DV_{level j}}{N}$$ Eq. 4.44

where f_o is the observed frequency in the sample for a given category and f_e is the frequency that would be expected based on the percentage in the population for a given category. Degrees of freedom are calculated by multiplying the number of categories of the independent variable – 1 by the number of categories of the dependent variable – 1 (df = (# of conditions of IV – 1)*(# of conditions of DV – 1)). The steps involved in computing a chi-square are summarized in Table 4.14.

Table 4.14   Steps to calculating a chi-square test of independence

1. State the null hypothesis
2. Calculate f_o
3. Calculate f_e
4. Calculate $\chi^2_{obtained}$
5. Determine the probability associated with $\chi^2_{obtained}$
6. Make a decision to reject or fail to reject the null hypothesis
7. Interpret the decision

Box 4.17   Conducting a chi-square analysis

Antarctica University wants to know if there are different proportions of men and women in computer science versus marketing versus history majors. It currently has 100 computer science majors, 50 marketing majors and 25 history majors. Of the 100 computer science majors, 70 are men and 30 are women. Of the 50 marketing majors, 40 are women and 10 are men. Of the 25 history majors, 20 are men and 5 are women.

Step 1: State the null hypothesis. The distribution of the majors is the same across men and women. Recall that although the null hypothesis is focused on the population, we use sample data to test the hypothesis and make inferences about the population.

Step 2: Calculate f_o. These values are simple counts listed below. In addition to the counts, one should create totals for each level of the IV and DV.

Step 3: Calculate f_e. Using Eq. 4.44, compute f_e for each cell in the table. These are based on the expected frequencies if the null is true based on a sample of the size of the present sample. The total across the category of the independent variable and the total across the category of the dependent variable are used in the calculation. Another way to think of this is the total of the column and the row to which the cell belongs. This can be done in Excel by manually entering Eq. 4.44:

	A	B	C	D	E	F	G	H
1	Observed							
2		Computer Science	Marketing	History	Total			
3	Men	70	10	20	100	Chi-square =	40.25 =sum(B14:D15)	
4	Women	30	40	5	75	p-value =	0.0000 = CHISQ.DIST(G3,G5,FALSE)	
5	Total	100	50	25	175	df=	2	
6								
7	Expected							
8		Computer Science	Marketing	History				
9	Men	57.14	28.57	14.29		=(B5*E3)/E5	=(C5*E3)/E5	=(D5*E3)/E5
10	Women	42.86	21.43	10.71		=(B5*E4)/E5	=(C5*E4)/E5	=(D5*E4)/E5
11								
12	Calculation for chi-square							
13		Computer Science	Marketing	History				
14	Men	2.89	12.07	2.29		=((B3-B9)^2)/B9	=((C3-C9)^2)/C9	=((D3-D9)^2)/D9
15	Women	3.86	16.10	3.05		=((B4-B10)^2)/B10	=((C4-C10)^2)/C10	=((D4-D10)^2)/D10

Notice that these numbers can be fractions, even if those fractions are not meaningful (i.e. it is impossible to have .5 of a person).

Step 4: Calculate $X^2_{obtained}$. Using Eq. 4.43, the χ^2 is computed. This is done in Excel using the 'sum' function = sum(f_e for each condition):

$$X^2_{obtained} = \Sigma \frac{(70-57.14)^2}{57.14}$$

$$= \frac{(10-28.57)^2}{28.57} + \frac{(20-14.29)^2}{14.28} + \frac{(30-42.86)^2}{42.85} + \frac{(40-21.43)^2}{21.42}$$

$$\frac{(5-10.71)^2}{10.71} = 2.89+12.07+2.29+3.86+16.10+3.05 = 40.25$$

Step 5: Determine the probability associated with $X^2_{obtained}$. The probability associated with the $X^2 = 40.25$ is <.001. This can be determined using the exact probability in a statistics program or using the critical value of 9.21 which is the X^2 value associated with a probability of .05. This is done in Excel using the 'chisq. dist' function = chisq.dist (X^2 value, df, FALSE).

Step 6: Make a decision to reject or fail to reject the null hypothesis. Based on the values of the test, one would reject the null hypothesis.

Step 7: Interpret the decision. The proportion of students in different majors does vary by gender. This means that the two variables are not independent of each other – there is an association between gender and major.

Other non-parametric quantitative analyses

There are a considerable number of other non-parametric tests that deserve some mention. There are several that can be used when there are two levels of the independent variable. The first is the Wilcoxon signed-rank test. This quantitative analysis examines differences in the ranks of paired variables similar to the Mann-Whitney U test. The resulting test statistic is compared to a z-distribution. The second is the sign test. This test utilizes the sign (i.e. $+$ or $-$) of the difference between a pair of variables (e.g. group 1 and group 2). The resulting test statistic is compared to a z-distribution for large samples or a binomial distribution for small samples. The third is the McNemar test, which is best used with experimental research designs. The McNemar test examines differences in the observed and expected change resulting from the experimental manipulation. The resulting test statistic is compared to a χ^2 distribution. Cochran's Q is the fourth test, which is useful when the dependent variable is a proportion. The resulting test statistic is compared to a χ^2 distribution.

If there are more than two levels of the independent variable, there are several different tests that can be used. First is the Kruskal Wallace test. This test uses the median to examine differences between groups in the ranks on the dependent variable. Second is the Friedman test. It can be used if there is a single independent variable that represents a repeated measure. This test also uses the median to examine differences in the ranks between groups. Post hoc tests are available for both the Kruskal Wallace and Friedman tests. Procedures for conducting these post hoc tests can be found in Gibbons (1993) or Siegel and Castellan (1998).

Part IV summary

Although quantitative tests that use data measured on an interval or ratio scale of measurement are typically the most statistically powerful, not all variables or research situations are conducive to these types of measures. In these cases, or when the distributional assumptions of parametric tests are not met, non-parametric tests can be used. There are a large number of non-parametric tests, but two of the more common tests in business and management studies are the Mann-Whitney U test and the chi-square test of independence. The Mann-Whitney U test provides information about the association between variables when both are measured on an ordinal scale (i.e. does the rank order on variable X have any association with the order on variable Y?). When dealing with nominal data, the chi-square test of independence is a suitable test. Based on the logic of comparing observed differences in frequencies to expected differences, the chi-square tests whether two variables are independent (i.e. there is no association) or if there is some association between membership in categories of the two nominal variables.

5

EXAMPLES OF
QUANTITATIVE DATA ANALYSIS

In this chapter, we present examples of published research that have used many of the quantitative analyses discussed in the previous chapter, including the independent t-test, single-factor independent ANOVA, repeated-measures ANOVA, two-factor independent ANOVA, linear regression, correlation, the Mann-Whitney U test and the chi-square test of independence. The studies that we review in this chapter utilize different research designs and sampling methods as well as illustrate how the quantitative analyses covered in this book are used and reported. Additionally, these articles are widely accessible for an independent review by the reader. For each paper, we review the hypotheses, sampling methods, research design, the quantitative analyses, the reasons for the choices made about the quantitative analyses and the appropriateness of those choices.

Example of an independent t-test and single-factor independent ANOVA

An example of an independent t-test and single-factor ANOVA comes from Sengupta and Gupta's (2012) study in *The International Journal of Human Resource Management*, which explored differences in the dimensions of reasons for attrition (i.e. voluntarily leaving the job) based on gender, age, education level and marital status for employees in the business process outsourcing (BPO) industry in India. In this study, no specific hypotheses about the nature of the differences were proposed. Instead, the authors noted that the study was exploratory in nature.

Sengupta and Gupta tested their exploratory research questions using a non-experimental research design in which a questionnaire was administered to 500 employees in the BPO industry in India. The sample was obtained through a simple random sampling of low and mid-level BPO industry employees. It should be noted that the authors do not define the sampling frame from which this simple random sample was obtained (i.e. all employees in the BPO industry in India or all employees in a single BPO organization in India).

The questionnaire included demographic questions (i.e. age, gender, education and marital status) and 21 questions to assess the importance of different factors that may lead to employee attrition. Each of the attrition questions was rated on a five-point rating scale with anchors that ranged from 'least important' to 'most important'. The data from the attrition questions can be considered to be on an interval scale of measurement. The responses to these 21 questions were then subjected to a confirmatory factor analysis and reduced to eight underlying dimensions or factors (hostile organizational culture, substandard nature of job, mystified career path, discontented personal factors, uncongenial organization support, dispirited perceptual factors, low self-fulfilment factors, unfavourable working conditions). Consistent with best practices, these measures are described in some detail in the article.

Sengupta and Gupta do not provide information about the presence of missing data or outliers. They report the means and standard deviations for each of the attrition dimensions. Frequency information is reported for the demographic variables. Age was measured as a ratio scale of measurement, but was converted to a nominal scale based on age categories (younger than 25, between 26 and 30, older than 30). The same process was followed with tenure (less than 1 year with the organization, 2-3 years, more than 3 years). All other variables were dichotomous (gender = male or female; marital status = married or unmarried; education = graduate or postgraduate) and on a nominal scale of measurement.

To test for mean differences in the attrition dimensions between the demographic groups, Sengupta and Gupta (2012) conducted several independent t-tests. In the first set of analyses, the independent variable was gender and the dependent variable was importance ratings of each of the eight attrition dimensions. As listed in Table 10 of the article, they found significant gender differences for five of the eight attrition dimensions. For example, they found that the females reported that the substandard nature of the job was more important in deciding to leave a job in the BPO industry on average than did males ($t = 4.27$, $p < 0.01$). However, males reported that discontented personal factors were more important in deciding to leave a job in the BPO industry on average than females ($t = 3.94$, $p < 0.01$). For the remaining three dimensions with statistically significant results, males reported that the dimension was more important in deciding to leave a job in the BPO industry on average than females. It is important to note that the authors did not report the degrees of freedom for their analyses. This information should be reported when communicating the results of a t-test.

The same process was followed for comparing unmarried to married respondents and postgraduate to graduate respondents, as listed in Tables 11 and 12 of the article. Sengupta and Gupta reported that there were statistically significant differences between married and unmarried employees in the importance of six of the dimensions in deciding to leave a job. With the exception of unfavourable working conditions, married employees reported that the dimension was more important in deciding to leave a job than unmarried employees. The authors also reported that there were statistically significant differences between the different levels of educational attainment for several of the attrition dimensions. The nature of these differences varied considerably (in some cases, graduates reported a dimension to be more important and in other cases postgraduates reported a dimension to be more important). These were the appropriate analyses given that the focus was comparing means of a dependent variable across two levels of a grouping or independent variable.

Because age was artificially recoded into three levels, it was assessed with a single-factor independent ANOVA and Duncan's post hoc test (see Table 13 of the article). This analysis was an appropriate choice given that there were more than two levels of the grouping or independent variable and the interest in mean differences. The authors reported that the F-test was statistically significant for five of the eight attrition dimensions. For example, the F-test indicated that there was a mean difference across the age groups in the importance of hostile organizational culture in deciding to leave a job ($F = 3.67$, $p < 0.05$). The Duncan's post hoc test revealed that those in the younger than 25 age group were statistically significantly different from the 26 to 30 age group and from the older than 30 age group, but that the 26 to 30 age group and the older than 30 age group were not statistically significantly different. The same process was followed with tenure as the independent variable and the results are presented in Table 14 of the article. It is important to note again that the authors did not report the degrees of freedom for the ANOVA analyses. This information should be reported when communicating the results of an ANOVA.

The authors reasonably interpret the results and offer some speculation for the patterns that the analyses revealed. The authors note only a few limitations of their study. They state that the study could be expanded 'to a larger area in a different zone altogether', although it is not clear what they mean by different zone (organizational context, time zone, etc.). They also note that using 21 questions to capture the vast set of reasons that may be part of one's decision to leave a job may be insufficient and that additional items should be included in future research to gain a more comprehensive picture of dimensions influencing attrition decisions. An additional limitation not mentioned by the authors is the treatment of age and tenure as nominal variables. These variables were measured on a ratio scale, but transformed to a nominal scale of measurement. Such a practice results in a loss of information (e.g. 60-year-olds are treated identically to 31-year-olds in the analysis) and can have a considerable impact on the results obtained from the analyses. A more appropriate method is to preserve the ratio scale of the data and analyse it using a correlation or regression analysis. These analyses would provide a better indication of the strength of association between age and tenure with the importance of the attrition dimensions. Additionally, there are some limitations related to the analyses. First, the authors did not report effect sizes, which would be useful in interpreting results. Second, the large number of t-tests conducted greatly compounds the *Type I error* rate, which is not mentioned nor addressed through corrections to the alpha value.

Example of a repeated-measures ANOVA

An example of a repeated-measures ANOVA comes from Walla, Brenner and Koller's (2011) study in *PLOS One* on the objective measurement of customers' emotional aspects of their attitudes toward consumer brands. Specifically, the authors were interested in which biological and physiological measures (e.g. eye blink, skin conductance and heart rate) could be used to capture an individual's emotionally-related aspects of an attitude (i.e. like or dislike) toward consumer brands. In this study, Walla et al. hypothesized that there would be differences in the frequency of eye blinks, mean level of skin conductance and mean level of heart rate for consumer brands that are liked versus those that are disliked.

To test their hypotheses, they conducted a multipart experimental study. The participants were 29 German adults who volunteered to be part of the study. This sample likely represents a convenience sample, but there is insufficient information to conclusively determine the sampling method. The authors note that eight participants were excluded from the analyses due to excessive missing data or no clear physiological response. In the first part of the study, the participants rated their like or dislike of 300 consumer brands common in Germany. They rated the brands on a 21-point electronic slider scale. Using these data, Walla et al. (2011) were able to identify the 10 most and least liked brands for each participant. These data represent an interval scale of measurement.

In the second part of the study, these individualized lists of most liked and disliked brands were used as the independent variables in which the visual presentation of the liked and disliked brands were presented as a within-subjects manipulation to the participants. Additionally, the order of presentation was randomized and filler items that were neutral in terms of like or dislike were presented. The dependent variables were the physiological measures of eye blinking, skin conductance and heart rate. Consistent with best practice, the authors provide detailed descriptions of the measures.

The authors provide a detailed description of the preparation of the data from the physiological measures, including a number of transformations that were executed on the data to prepare them for analysis. These measures represent a ratio scale of measurement. In the text of the results section, Walla et al. mention the means and standard deviation of the physiological measures but do not provide an interpretation of them. As is common practice, no additional measures of central tendency or variability are noted.

To test their hypotheses about the impact of the emotional reaction to the brands on the physiological measures, Walla et al. (2011) conducted several repeated-measures ANOVAs with the liked or disliked brands as the repeated factors and the physiological measures as the dependent variables. In this case, a repeated-measures ANOVA was appropriate given the data for the dependent variable was measured on a ratio scale of and the participants were included in all levels of the independent variable. They found a statistically significant difference between the liked and disliked brands in the mean number of eye blinks (F = 5.110, p = 0.035, η^2 = 0.203) such that eye blinking was more frequent for disliked brands than for liked brands. They found a statistically significant difference between the liked and disliked brands in the mean level of skin conductance (F = 12.581, p = 0.002, η^2 = 0.386) such that there was greater skin conductance response to disliked brands than liked brands. However, the analysis of the heart rate data did not reach statistical significance (F = 3.970, p = 0.060, η^2 = 0.166), but the pattern of the means showed a lower heart rate for liked brands than for disliked brands. It is important to note that the authors did not report the degrees of freedom for their analyses. This information should be reported when communicating the results of an ANOVA. However, the authors did report effect sizes for their analyses which is consistent with best practice.

In interpreting their results, Walla et al. carefully note the potential of the biological and physiological measures as additional measures of emotional aspects of brand attitudes while situating their findings in the context of the previous literature. They note possible caveats and limitations in their data such as the large within-group standard deviations and possible questions about the construct validity of their measures. They do make some causal interpretations of the results of their quantitative analyses, which are appropriate given the experimental research design.

Example of a two-factor independent ANOVA

Study 1 of Grant's (2012) article in the *Academy of Management Journal* illustrates the use of a two-factor independent ANOVA. The goal of the study was to assess whether the effectiveness of a transformational leader in motivating followers (i.e. enhancing their performance) depends on whether the followers are able to interact with internal or external customers who are directly benefiting from their work products. The specific hypothesis that was tested using a two-factor independent ANOVA was that contact with a beneficiary of an employee's work product will strengthen the relationship between transformational leadership and followers' performance.

Grant tested this question using a quasi-experimental research design conducted in the field with a sample of 71 recently hired call centre employees. The sample was selected from a single organization and all recently hired employees participated.

Although it is not explicitly stated, we assume this is a convenience sample. The two independent variables in the study were exposure to transformational leadership (exposed or not exposed) and contact with a beneficiary of an employee's work product (contact or no contact). In total, there were four conditions (exposed to transformational leader and beneficiary contact; not exposed to transformational leader but exposed to beneficiary contact; exposed to transformational leader but not exposed to beneficiary contact, and not exposed to transformational leader or beneficiary contact). These variables were manipulated through the inclusion or exclusion of the presenter speaking about content related to transformational leadership and beneficiary contact during a mandatory training session for recently hired employees. There were four training sessions, and each served as one of the four conditions. Employees were able to choose which of the four sessions they would attend. The employee self-selection in one of the four conditions represents the assignment to conditions. Thus, the assignment to conditions was not random and makes this study a quasi-experiment. The dependent variable was the employees' performance, which was operationalized as the number of sales transactions and the total revenue generated over the seven weeks after the manipulation. Both of these dependent variables are on a ratio scale of measurement.

The author does not provide information about the presence of missing data or outliers. The means and standard deviations for each condition are provided in Table 1 of the article. As is common practice, no additional measures of central tendency or variability are noted. To test the hypothesis, a two-factor ANOVA was conducted. This analysis is an appropriate choice given that there are two independent variables being simultaneously compared on a single dependent variable and that the focus of the hypothesis is on the interaction between these two independent variables. There was no statistically significant main effect of transformational leadership ($F(1,66) = 0.01$, $p = 0.93$) or beneficiary contact ($F(1,66) = 0.26$, $p = 0.69$) on sales, but there was a significant interaction effect ($F(1,66) = 7.73$, $p < 0.01$). A similar pattern was observed with revenue with no statistically significant main effect of transformational leadership ($F(1,66) = 0.00$, $p > 0.99$) or beneficiary contact ($F(1,66) = 0.13$, $p = 0.77$) and a significant interaction effect ($F(1,66) = 4.67$, $p < 0.05$). The pattern of interaction is displayed in Figures 1 and 2 of the article. The figures show that when there was beneficiary contact, transformational leadership had an effect on sales and revenue (but only if a one-tailed test is used). When there was no contact, transformational leadership did not have an effect on sales or revenue.

Grant (2012) is appropriately careful in interpreting his results in line with the study design. He admits that the quasi-experimental design is vulnerable to validity threats, particularly larger events occurring in the company and economy at the same time as the experimental manipulation treatment that could impact on the data on the performance measures. He also considers possible alternative interpretations of the findings, including the possibility of the results stemming from the number of speakers during the training instead of from the specific content about which they spoke. He also mentions limitations surrounding the short nature of the training intervention and the generalizability of results outside of the call centre job context. Nonetheless, he suggests that his results do provide evidence in support of the hypothesis that beneficiary contact strengthens the effects of transformational leadership on followers' performance. Also important to consider is that the author did not report effect sizes, which would be useful in interpreting results, and the author switches between one- and two-tailed tests in conducting the analyses.

Example of correlation and ordinary least squares regression

An example of correlation and regression analyses comes from Lee, Wong, Foo and Leung's (2011) study in the *Journal of Business Venturing* on the individual and organizational factors that can predict entrepreneurial intentions. Specifically, they were interested in how job satisfaction, innovation climate, innovation orientation and technical excellence incentives were related to individuals' intention to leave their job to start their own business. They hypothesized that innovation climate and technical excellence incentives would predict job satisfaction. In turn, job satisfaction and innovation orientation would predict intentions to leave one's job and start a new business.

To examine these relationships, Lee et al. utilized a secondary data source that was collected as part of a non-experimental study. The secondary data source included survey questions on individuals' job satisfaction, perceptions of their organization's innovation climate, perceptions about technical excellence incentives, individuals' reported innovation orientation and intentions to leave the current job to start a new business. These survey questions were rated on a five-point response scale with the anchors of strongly disagree and strongly agree. Thus, these data represent an interval scale of measurement. Consistent with best practice, the authors provide descriptions of the measures. A stratified sampling approach was used to select participants to complete the questionnaire. It is not noted in the article whether the sampling within each stratum was random. The final sample consisted of 4,192 IT professionals based in Singapore.

Table 4 of the article reports the measures of central tendency and variability. The means for all of the survey items were near the mid-point of the response scale, indicating the sample in general was roughly neutral on these variables. The standard deviations indicate that there is variability in the responses, but the variability is relatively small. The mean and standard deviation are the only measures of central tendency and variability reported. However, it is common practice to only report these two measures in journal articles.

Table 4 of the article reports the correlations between the variables in the study. Lee et al. (2011) found that innovation climate showed a statistically significant negative correlation with entrepreneurial intentions ($r = -0.18$, $p < 0.05$) and a statistically significant positive correlation with job satisfaction ($r = 0.09$, $p < 0.05$).

These correlations indicate that the stronger the belief that one's organization had a climate of innovation, the lower the reported intentions of leaving to start a new business and the higher the reported job satisfaction. They also found a statistically significant negative correlation between technical excellence incentive and entrepreneurial intentions ($r = -0.17$, $p < 0.05$) and a statistically significant positive correlation with job satisfaction ($r = 0.08$, $p < 0.05$). These correlations indicate that the stronger the belief that one's organization had technical excellence incentives, the lower the reported intentions of leaving to start a new business and the higher the reported job satisfaction. There was a statistically significant negative correlation between innovation orientation and entrepreneurial intentions ($r = 0.14$, $p < 0.05$), but the correlation between innovation orientation and job satisfaction was not statistically significant ($r = 0.04$, $p > 0.05$). The correlation between entrepreneurial intentions and job satisfaction was negative and statistically significant ($r = -0.32$, $p < 0.05$), indicating that higher levels of job satisfaction were associated with lower intentions of leaving to start a new business. Given that all of the data can be treated on an interval scale of measurement and the interest in relationships, correlations were an appropriate analysis.

Table 5 of the article reports a series of regression analyses to test the study's primary hypotheses. Given the authors' interest in predicting job satisfaction and entrepreneurial intentions, as well as the availability of data on an interval scale of measurement, regression is an appropriate analysis. Models 2 and 4 in Table 5 are representative of multiple regression analyses. In model 2, they included a number of control variables in the model related to age and experience, in addition to the primary variables of organizational innovation climate, technical excellence incentives and innovation orientation to predict job satisfaction. The purpose of the control variables was to remove any variance that could mask the relationship between the primary variables. This is the same idea as when a partial correlation is used to remove variance attributable to a third variable. They found that after controlling for age- and experience-related variables, organizational innovation climate ($b = 2.115$, $p < 0.05$) and technical excellence incentives ($b = 1.769$, $p < 0.05$) were statistically significant predictors of job satisfaction. The results indicate that a one-point increase in organizational innovation climate predicts a 2.115 increase in job satisfaction and a one-point increase in technical excellence incentives predicts a 1.769 increase in job satisfaction. Interestingly, innovation orientation demonstrated a negative and statistically significant relationship with job satisfaction ($b = -1.000$, $p < 0.05$), but it demonstrated a positive and non-significant correlation with job satisfaction.

Situations such as this one where a regression coefficient demonstrates a sign that is opposite of the correlation and becomes significant in regression (but is not significant in the correlation analysis) are indicative of a suppression effect (see Tzelgov and Henik, 1991). Suppression effects are a statistical artefact that can occur in regression where the predictors are correlated (i.e. multicollinearity) and as a result suppress variance in one another which changes the nature of the relationship with the criterion. The authors discuss the correlations and the possibility of multicollinearity impacting on the results. They argue that multicollinearity is not impacting on the results, but do not discuss the suppression effect that is apparent in the regression analysis.

In model 4, Lee et al. included a number of control variables related to age and experience in the model in addition to the primary variables of organizational innovation climate, technical excellence incentives and innovation to predict entrepreneurial intentions. They found that after controlling for age- and experience-related variables, organizational innovation climate ($b = -1.135$, $p < .05$) and technical excellence incentives ($b = -1.129$, $p < .05$) were statistically significant predictors of entrepreneurial intentions. The results indicate that a one-point decrease in organizational innovation climate predicts a 1.135 decrease in entrepreneurial intentions and a one-point increase in technical excellence incentives predicts a 1.129 decrease in entrepreneurial intentions. Innovation orientation demonstrated a positive and statistically significant relationship with entrepreneurial intentions ($b = 1.013$, $p < .05$), which is consistent with the correlation. This result indicates that a one-point increase in innovation orientation predicts a 1.013 increase in entrepreneurial intentions.

In interpreting their results, the authors are careful to describe the nature of the relationship in terms that do not imply causality. As is true in most non-experimental studies, some terms are used that could imply causality such as 'influence'. For example, the use of the term influence in the article's title implies that the individual and organizational factors cause entrepreneurial intentions. Although Lee et al. (2011) give careful and appropriate interpretations that are consistent with their data, it is a reminder that all researchers need to be thoughtful in interpreting their results consistent with the nature of their data, scale of measurement and research design. Lee et al. are also careful not to generalize the results beyond the IT industry. As they note in their limitations section, additional research would be needed to extend the results to other industries.

Example of a Mann-Whitney U test

Qayyum and Sukirno's (2012) study in *Global Business and Management Research: An International Journal* investigates differences in the relative importance and availability of various motivational factors for banking industry employees in Pakistan. The authors do not propose specific hypotheses about which motivational factors they believe will be most important. Rather, they frame the study as exploratory in nature because most previous research on employee motivation has been conducted in developed countries in North America and Europe. Therefore, this study tested the extent to which these findings are generalizable to less developed countries such as Pakistan.

To test their exploratory research questions, Qayyum and Sukirno conducted a non-experimental study in which they administered a questionnaire to employees in banks in Islamabad, Pakistan. The authors employed a cluster sampling strategy, such that they randomly selected three banks from the 39 in Pakistan and then administered the questionnaire to all employees in these three banks. Of the 200 questionnaires that were sent to bank employees, 165 were completed and returned (an 83% response rate). The questionnaire asked participants to rank order 12 motivational factors (high salary, seniority-based promotions, chance to benefit society, personal development/learning, a stable and secure future, balanced work and family life, physical working environment, opportunity for advancement, social status/prestige, fringe benefits, relaxed working environment, benefits after retirement) in order of importance, with 1 being the most important. They also rank ordered the same factors in terms of availability in their current jobs. Both of these variables are ranks and on an ordinal scale of measurement. The authors also collected information on the gender and educational status of the employees. Both were nominal scales of measurement. There is no mention of the occurrence of missing data or outliers.

The authors were interested in whether the rank order of the motivational factors in terms of their importance differed significantly by gender and educational attainment (bachelors versus masters degree). To test this question, the authors conducted a series of Mann-Whitney U tests and report the results in Table 4 of the article. For the male and female comparisons, the z-statistic was only significant for seniority-based promotions ($z = -2.415$, $p = 0.016$) with male employees ranking this motivational factor as more important than did female employees. This same process was followed for education (also listed in Table 4 of the article), with significant differences emerging between a stable and secure future and opportunity for advancement (both ranked higher by those with bachelors degrees than those with masters degrees).

The authors appropriately interpret their results and describe the potential implications of their findings. They are careful to describe their findings in terms of significant differences without implying causality. Given the non-experimental nature of the study, causal interpretations would be inappropriate. They note limitations of their study including that generalizing to contexts outside of a developing country in Asia and to industries other than banking is not supported by their findings. However, they do not mention that the large number of statistical tests conducted greatly compounds the *Type I error* rate or address the issue through corrections to the alpha value.

Example of a chi-square test of independence

An example of a chi-square test of independence comes from Griskevicius, Tybur and Van den Bergh's (2010) study in the *Journal of Personality and Social Psychology* on consumers' motivations for purchasing environmentally-friendly products.

Specifically, they conducted a number of studies to examine how the motive for status and reputation influences choices for luxury non-environmentally-friendly products vs. non-luxury environmentally-friendly products. For the purposes of demonstrating a chi-square analysis, we focus on study one of the article. Based on a number of psychological and economic theories, Griskevicius et al. hypothesized that when the motivation for status was activated, the choice of non-luxury environmentally-friendly products would be more frequent than the choice of luxury non-environmentally-friendly products.

To test the hypotheses of study one, Griskevicius et al. (2010) conducted an experimental study. The participants were 168 undergraduate college students. This sample represents a convenience sample. Participants were randomly assigned to a condition where the motivation for status was activated using a priming technique (e.g. reading a story with strong status themes) or to a condition where status motivation was not primed (i.e. control condition). Once the participant's status motive was manipulated, they were asked to consider shopping for three different products (i.e. a car, a household cleaner and a dishwasher). Although not reviewed here, the authors conducted a substantial amount of testing before conducting the experiment to ensure the effectiveness of the motive for status manipulation and the comparability of the products. For each product type, participants were asked to choose between two equally-priced options with one being a luxury non-environmentally-friendly product and the other being a non-luxury environmentally-friendly product. These data represent a nominal scale of measurement as they represent a dichotomous choice.

Figure 1 of the article reports the percentage of participants choosing the non-luxury environmentally-friendly product over the luxury non-environmentally-friendly product in each condition. Given that the independent variable was a dichotomous variable and the dependent variables were counts of categories, the data are on a nominal scale of measurement and a chi-square test of independence is an appropriate analysis. Griskevicius et al. report that in the control condition, 37.2% chose the environmentally-friendly car, 25.7% chose the environmentally-friendly household cleaner and 34.5% chose the environmentally-friendly dishwasher. In the status motive condition, 54.5% chose the environmentally-friendly car, 41.8% chose the environmentally-friendly household cleaner and 49.1% chose the environmentally-friendly dishwasher. The chi-square analysis indicated that there was a significant association between the condition and product choice. The choice of the environmentally-friendly car, χ^2 (1, N = 168) = 4.56, p = .033, and the environmentally-friendly household cleaner, χ^2 (1, N = 168) = 4.52, p = .034, were more frequent in the status motive condition than in the control condition. For the environmentally-friendly dishwasher, the results did not reach statistical significance, χ^2 (1, N = 168) = 3.30, p = .069.

Griskevicius et al. (2010) discuss their findings in a way that implied that the hypotheses were supported for all three products. Although we agree with that interpretation, the data do not strictly support the hypothesis concerning the dishwasher. However, when the results are taken as a set, they do support the conclusion that non-luxury environmentally-friendly products are selected more often when a status motive is active than when it is not active. These findings demonstrate the importance of examining the pattern of results across the quantitative analyses in addition to examining the results of each quantitative analysis in isolation. An individual quantitative analysis may not support a hypothesis, but a set of them may reveal a pattern supportive of the hypothesis.

Griskevicius et al. describe the nature of the findings as supporting causality. In this study, these interpretations are appropriate given that the data were collected using a randomized experimental design. In the general discussion of the article, the authors explicitly consider alternative interpretations of the data and rule them out. The process of ruling out alternative explanations is a key factor in establishing evidence to support causal conclusions. Griskevicius et al. (2010) also consider a number of potential limitations to their findings. One that we would add is a consideration of the sample and its representativeness. The authors indirectly consider this factor when noting that there was no actual choice, just a hypothetical one. However, the concern needs additional elaboration. The sample likely consisted of American college students with little experience of making these types of decisions. Thus, the degree to which this sample is representative of individuals making these purchase decisions is unknown. Also, the generalizability to other populations (e.g. non-American consumers) is unknown at this point. Although Griskevicius et al. are appropriate, thorough and thoughtful in their interpretations of their data, the importance of careful consideration of the implications of the sample for the interpretation of quantitative analyses cannot be understated.

SUMMARY

To illustrate the use of many of the quantitative analyses described in this book, we reviewed a number of published business and management studies using them. In particular, studies using the independent t-test, the single-factor independent ANOVA, the repeated-measures ANOVAs, the two-factor independent ANOVAs, ordinary least squares regression, correlation, the Mann-Whitney U test and the chi-square test of independence are discussed. For each study, we focused on the research design, the sampling method, the quantitative analyses used, the appropriateness of those analyses and the nature of the conclusions drawn from the analyses. These studies provide a reasonable representation of how these analyses are commonly reported and the types of situations where the analyses are appropriate.

6

CONCLUSIONS

In the previous chapters, we have considered the epistemological foundations of quantitative analyses, the basic components needed for quantitative analyses, many of the quantitative analyses used with experimental and non-experimental research, and reviewed published examples using these analyses. In this chapter, we consider the strengths and limitations of quantitative analyses as well as criteria that can be used to evaluate quantitative analyses. When considering both the strengths and limitations, it is important to remember that these are simply the possible strengths and limitations. The use of quantitative analyses does not guarantee that the research will benefit from the strengths or suffer due to the limitations. The researcher will need to evaluate both in every application of quantitative analysis. This evaluation should occur before the research commences, as well as when the analyses are complete, to ensure that there is an alignment between the hypothesis, the research design, the quantitative analyses and the desired conclusions (Aguinis and Edwards, 2014; Aguinis and Vandenberg, 2014). When considering the strengths and limitations, it is important to consider them in the context of a research design. Ultimately, quantitative analyses cannot compensate for or overcome a poor research design. However, they can certainly benefit from a strong research design.

STRENGTHS OF QUANTITATIVE ANALYSES

Each type of quantitative analysis has a number of benefits related to the specific purpose of the analyses, as detailed in Chapter 4, but there are also a number of general strengths of quantitative analyses. Their potential strengths primarily involve making decisions about hypotheses and research questions as well as communicating those tests of hypotheses and research questions.

A primary strength of quantitative analyses is that they offer a structured process for making systematic decisions about research questions and hypotheses based on data (Abelson, 1995). In other words, they provide a set of rules for how hypotheses should be evaluated. In order to claim support for a hypothesis, a researcher must obtain data and rigorously analyse that data using a standardized set of steps. Although there are some criticisms (see Harlow et al., 1997 or Shrout, 1997), the null hypothesis significance testing process, especially when combined with other evidence such as effect sizes and statistical power, helps minimize the likelihood of supporting true null hypotheses and failing to support false null hypotheses.

Quantitative analyses provide a standardized and agreed-on system for researchers to communicate the process they used to examine their data (Scherbaum, 2005). When a researcher notes that a t-test was conducted on data from an experimental study, other researchers can have a fairly specific and detailed idea of what was done to the data and the nature of the conclusions that are appropriate. For example, if a researcher reports that the p-value of a t-test was 0.20, other researchers know that rejecting the null hypothesis is not an appropriate conclusion. Also, this standardized communication facilitates the accumulation of research findings into meta-analyses and research synthesis methods.

It is important to note that the use of quantitative analysis limits, but does not eliminate, the subjectivity in making judgements about the support of hypotheses. Several steps in the quantitative analysis process involve choices, such as the decision to remove outliers, the decision to use a one- or two-tailed test, the decision of where to set the alpha level and the decision about which extraneous variables should be included as covariates. Although these choices inherently imply subjectivity, quantitative analyses typically are conducted and reported in a manner that creates transparency about these choices, which has several benefits. First, it facilitates the opportunity for other researchers to independently evaluate the degree to which the analyses and conclusions about the support of hypotheses are reasonable and appropriate. Second, this transparency also allows other researchers to replicate each others' analyses using the same data or different data. The capacity to evaluate and compare both exact and conceptual replications is critical for the scientific progress of any field and for the development of a field's theories. Research questions and hypotheses that cannot be independently replicated lose support in the field; those that can be continuously replicated gain support and are further studied. Lastly, having clear decision points helps ensure that there is a degree of self-monitoring and correction in a field of study. Studies making choices and inferences that are not deemed to be appropriate by peers in a field are unlikely to be disseminated in the recognized outlets in a given field.

The use of quantitative analyses is consistent with the 'evidence-based' movement in a number of fields that increasingly rely on quantitatively analysed data as the basis of recommendations and practice decisions (Pfeffer and Sutton, 2006). Quantitative analyses provide an alternative to relying on case studies, anecdotes and limited personal experience as a means of evidence. They also provide a way for decision-makers to identify the 'good' evidence from the plethora of published and online material devoted to business and management issues. Evidence that is supported by quantitative analysis provides the decision-maker with a means to evaluate the results and helps ensure that they were not achieved by chance. With the use of ordinary least squares regression analyses, decision-makers are also able to easily transfer findings and make predictions based on local data. Additionally, through the use of certain quantitative analyses (such as interaction effects), decision-makers are better able to pinpoint contextual factors that may impact on the effectiveness of certain interventions, policies or programs. When using evidence derived from other business or organizational contexts, this is very important as it can facilitate decisions about whether such interventions, policies or programs are likely to be successful within one's own particular business or organizational circumstances.

LIMITATIONS OF QUANTITATIVE ANALYSES

Although there are a number of strengths of quantitative analyses, they are not without their potential limitations. Their potential limitations primarily involve the requirements for using quantitative analyses and whether these requirements are met in any given application of quantitative analyses. As discussed in Chapter 2, quantitative analyses are primarily limited to epistemological perspectives that support the generalization of the sample data to the population and that data can be aggregated across individuals. Thus, the use of quantitative analysis requires one to take some degree of a post-positivist perspective or at least some of the key elements of it, such as the position that there can be an objective reality. Thus, quantitative analyses are limited to situations where the researcher is asking research questions consistent with post-positivist and some interpretive perspectives (e.g. symbolic interaction). Researchers not wishing to take these perspectives may want to consider other approaches to analysing and interpreting data.

Related to the perspective taken is that all quantitative analyses require that the data be quantitative and the different analyses place different requirements on the nature of the data. If the data are qualitative (e.g. narratives, interview notes, descriptive observations), they are not appropriate for quantitative analyses unless they are quantified in some manner, such as through content analysis or text mining. However, it is important to keep in mind that quantifying inherently qualitative data may not be consistent with the epistemological perspective of the research or may remove important contextual aspects of the data. Additionally, some research questions are simply more conducive to qualitative data or greatly benefit from the use of qualitative data as a starting point to later guide quantitative questions. For example, if an organization wishes to better understand why employees are quitting, exit interviews are a very useful source of information. After gathering data from several interviews, a researcher is likely to gain a better idea of variables to include in quantitative analyses in the future (e.g. if many people mention salary as a reason for leaving, then salary can be quantitatively analysed in relation to turnover to see if there is indeed a quantitative link between the variables). Thus, the use of quantitative methods alone may sometimes be too broad and qualitative research may serve as an initial guiding resource. In addition to requiring that the data be quantitative, most analyses require that the data take a particular scale of numerical measurement. The majority of the analyses covered in this book require the data for the dependent variable to be measured using an interval or ratio scale of measurement. Some types of data are not amenable to this measurement form.

The majority of the quantitative analyses covered in this book require the researcher to make some assumptions about the distribution of the dependent variable, and in some cases independent variable, in the population. Although the specific assumptions and test of those assumptions were not covered in great detail here, they are a critical part of quantitative analysis. For example, many quantitative analyses make a number of different assumptions including that the variables are normally distributed in the population, the variances of the groups being compared are equal in the population or the relationships between the variables are linear. Diagnostic tests of the viability of these assumptions are included in most statistical software. However, many of these diagnostic tests require some subjectivity as there are no definitive rules or guidelines for what constitutes the assumptions being met. Given that the outcome of these diagnostic tests is a determinant of whether it is appropriate to conduct the quantitative analysis, this source of subjectivity has considerable implications. A researcher needs to carefully consider the outcomes of those tests to determine whether it is appropriate to continue the analysis and interpret the results of the quantitative analysis and, if appropriate, how strongly to make those interpretations. The researcher should also clearly communicate the choices made so that they can be evaluated by other researchers.

Although the standardization inherent in quantitative analyses is considered a strength, it is not without limitations. Within null hypothesis significance testing, researchers set firm rules a priori about acceptable probability values for rejecting the null hypothesis (i.e. the alpha level). If alpha is set at .05, an obtained probability value of .052 would result in failure to reject the null hypothesis, whereas an obtained probability of .048 in another study would result in rejection of the null hypothesis. In reality, the results of these two studies are quite similar, but very different conclusions may be drawn (e.g. an intervention is successful or not). For this reason, we urge researchers to also use effect sizes in conjunction with null hypothesis significance testing and to carefully consider whether the sample size of the study provides appropriate power to avoid *Type II errors*. Relatedly, the process of null hypothesis significance testing necessitates *Type I error*; thus, in any given study there is a chance that the null will be falsely rejected. We urge replication of quantitative analyses in multiple samples to help assuage this issue.

Finally, the focus of quantitative analyses is sets or groups of individuals, not individual cases. Although descriptive quantitative analyses can be used on repeated measurements from a *single* individual, inferential quantitative analyses are not appropriate on a single individual (they would be appropriate if there were groups of individuals). With the exception of regression analyses, none of the analyses provides information about a given individual. They provide information about what is typical for the group that an individual belongs to. Additionally, quantitative analyses also require sample sizes that are greater than 10 and much larger in most cases. Samples of these sizes are not available for some populations and some research questions. In these cases, inferential quantitative analyses are not an option.

EVALUATING QUANTITATIVE ANALYSES

The effective planning and execution of a research study is a product of the many choices that have been described throughout this book. Researchers should carefully evaluate these choices at each step of a research study to ensure the results that are ultimately achieved can be used to test the study's hypotheses (Aguinis and Vandenberg, 2014; Aguinis et al., 2010; Buchanan and Bryman, 2007). In addition to evaluating the research during the planning process, researchers need to carefully evaluate their research once it is complete. At this stage, the evaluation focuses less on the choices and more on the implications of those choices for the results of the study and the appropriateness of the interpretations drawn from those results as well as the specific limitations of the quantitative analyses chosen. The importance of this type of evaluation cannot be understated as the use of quantitative analyses is outpacing the expertise on how to appropriately use and interpret quantitative analyses. Thus, results of quantitative analyses can easily be misinterpreted by those who do not have a deep expertise.

There are numerous criteria that can be used to evaluate research and quantitative analyses once they have been completed (e.g. Campion, 1993; Desrosiers et al., 2002). Some criteria are straightforward, such as whether the analysis selected is appropriate for the data and whether the analyses are capable of producing results that are relevant to the research question. Other criteria are less obvious. This chapter focuses on several of these less obvious criteria that we recommend researchers carefully consider when evaluating their research, quantitative analyses and inferences drawn from those analyses.

Philosophical and theoretical criteria

As discussed in Chapter 2 and earlier in this chapter, researchers need to carefully consider the ontological and epistemological position they have taken and how that may be compatible with quantitative analysis in general and descriptive or inferential quantitative analysis in particular. This also applies to the interpretation of the results from the quantitative analyses. The interpretations should be consistent with those permitted by the perspective adopted. If a perspective does not support generalizations, then the interpretations of the quantitative analyses should be descriptive in nature about the given sample (see Table 2.1). For example, hermeneutic perspectives do not support generalizing conclusions beyond the context in which the data was collected. Therefore, inferential quantitative analyses that were designed to do this are not compatible. As another example, critical realism can be compatible with both descriptive and inferential quantitative analyses when the data are objective properties that do not require subjective judgement. Otherwise, it is not compatible. Researchers should evaluate the degree to which the quantitative analyses that have been used will permit those types of comparisons (see Table 2.1).

Researchers should also evaluate their research in terms of the grounding of the interpretations of the quantitative analyses in theory. While quantitative analyses can always produce a result, the meaning of those results depends on the theory that the research was designed to test. However, research can often lead to unexpected or counterintuitive findings. In these cases, there will be a temptation to seek a theory to fit the observed patterns in the data (i.e. post hoc theorizing). There will also be the temptation to conduct every possible analysis when the initially planned analyses are not statistically significant. We strongly encourage researchers to avoid engaging in post hoc theorizing and 'fishing' with their data. These types of efforts may occasionally lead to insights that are novel and generalize over replications of the research. In most cases, they will lead to research that capitalizes on chance and cannot be replicated. This type of research holds little value for the progress of business and management research.

Statistical conclusion validity

Statistical conclusion validity is concerned with the appropriateness of the inferences about the nature of the relationship between the independent variable and the dependent variable (i.e. Austin et al., 1998; Cook and Campbell, 1979). In evaluating the statistical conclusion validity of their research study, researchers should consider a number of specific factors. First is the possibility of *Type I* and *Type II errors*. For example, researchers should consider the obtained statistical power of the tests as opposed to the a priori statistical power calculations discussed in Chapter 3. The actual power of the quantitative analyses may be much more or less than that estimated in the planning stages of the study. If one failed to reject the null hypothesis, was low statistical power one of the reasons for that decision? When samples are small and effect sizes are large, the impact of low statistical power deserves serious consideration. Has there been adequate consideration of the compounding effect of *Type I errors*? If 20 *t*-tests were performed, the probability of at least one *Type I error* is 1.0. Were steps taken to manage the overall *Type I error* rate, such as using quantitative analyses that help control the error rate or adjustment to the statistical significance level?

Second, as discussed earlier in this chapter, is the viability of the assumptions of the quantitative analysis. Third is the quality of the measurement of the variables. The reliability of the scores from the measures can have a considerable impact on the interpretation of quantitative analyses. If the scores from the measures demonstrate low levels of reliability, interpretations should be made very cautiously, if at all. Researchers should also consider the degree of restriction in the range of variables that may exist in the data. The presence of restriction of range typically serves to attenuate the magnitude of the obtained test results but can serve to increase the magnitude.

Fourth, researchers should consider the basis of conclusions about the null hypothesis. Was only the statistical significance test used or were multiple pieces of information used? As noted in Chapter 2, effect sizes, statistical power and confidence intervals should be used in addition to statistical significance tests.

Research method and design criteria

As described in Chapter 3, the design and method of the research study have a considerable impact on the nature of the conclusions that can be made. Causal interpretations are only possible from experimental designs. As noted in Chapter 5, it is not uncommon to see non-experimental research describe the findings in 'causal-like' terms. For example, terms such as 'influenced by', 'attributable to' or 'can be explained by' are frequently used to describe the relationship between independent and dependent variables. Researchers need to carefully consider what types of conclusions are permissible for the specific research design and what types of conclusions have been made. One should ensure that they are aligned.

Related to this factor is the degree to which the quantitative analyses and design have ruled out alternative explanations for the observed patterns in the data. For example, have third variables that could be responsible for an observed relationship been tested to the degree possible and ruled out? Have uncontrolled factors that could influence the dependent variable been considered and tested? Particularly with non-experimental research, alternative explanations can rarely be ruled out completely. Researchers should take all possible steps to test the likelihood of these alternatives to build confidence in the inferences that the researcher wishes to make. Also, researchers should consider the alignment between the nature of the phenomena of interest and the quantitative analyses. Many research questions in business and management research involve dynamic processes that unfold over time. Not all quantitative analyses are well suited to examining dynamic processes. For example, dynamic processes show a pattern called autocorrelation where observations from one point in time are related to the previous and next observations in time. That is, they are not independent observations. Many quantitative analyses assume that the observations are independent of one another. Researchers should carefully consider the alignment between the theoretical process, the research design and quantitative analysis to ensure that the interpretations are in alignment with what can be supported by the design and analysis.

Researchers should also carefully evaluate the nature of the inferences and generalizations from the quantitative analyses in terms of the nature of the sample and any limitations to the research design. In terms of the sample, researchers should consider whether the inferences to the population are supported by the sample. This is essentially a question of sample representativeness. Representativeness should be evaluated in terms of the characteristics of the sample and the research question. For example, some research questions focus on basic processes common to all individuals (e.g. emotional regulation under stress). In these cases, a variety of samples can be appropriate (e.g. university students). Other research questions are contextual and require very specific samples (e.g. how top management makes decisions about M&A activity). Research is often evaluated in terms of the sample characteristics only and negative reactions follow when particular samples are used (e.g. university students; Greenberg, 1987). Researchers should carefully consider the inferences that can be made from the sample, given the research question. Likewise, all research has limitations. There is no perfect research study. Thus, the results of a quantitative analysis should be interpreted in light of the limitations. For example, if an unexpected confound is introduced into an experimental research study, interpretations of causality need to be made in a manner consistent with that confound.

Other criteria

In addition to the conceptual, quantitative and design criteria, there are a number of more general criteria that all researchers need to consider. First, all researchers have a bias in interpreting their research that needs to be recognized. The bias is the desire to find support for the study's research hypotheses. One needs to evaluate their interpretation, especially when the results are ambiguous, to determine the degree to which the desired interpretation is given preference over other equally viable interpretations. We can never fully eliminate this bias but can minimize it by carefully considering it and taking steps to reduce its impact.

Researchers should also consider ethical dimensions to conducting and interpreting the results of quantitative analyses. Researchers should accurately report the results of their quantitative analyses and avoid manipulating the data to produce the desired result. A researcher can use quantitative analyses to support any hypothesis with enough manipulation of the data (Huff, 1954). The researcher has an ethical duty to faithfully report the actual steps taken in the quantitative analyses, the choices made and the support for the hypotheses. Given that there is an extreme preference for research that rejects the null hypothesis, large and small ethical breaches are possible and need to be guarded against.

Interpretation of quantitative analyses can be made along two dimensions. The first is the statistical significance. That is, were the hypotheses supported? The second is the practical significance. That is, what do the results mean for the world at large? Practical significance is often associated with the effect size for the quantitative analyses conducted. However, the magnitude of the effect size does not make a finding automatically practically meaningful. There are many cases where small effect sizes are extremely important (Abelson, 1985; Prentice and Miller, 1992). For example, if the effect size for a drug to treat cancer were increased by 0.50%, countless days could be added to patients' lives.

In many cases, there will be an alignment between the decision about the null hypothesis and the effect size. For example, there will be a large effect size and one rejects the null hypothesis. In such cases, decisions about the practical significance are fairly straightforward. It becomes more difficult in situations where the statistical significance and effect size are not aligned. A famous example of this situation is the original medical studies examining the impact of taking aspirin on the occurrence of heart attacks. The results were not statistically significant (due to the small sample size), but the effect size was exceptionally large. The researchers decided to base their conclusion on the effect size in this case. Researchers should carefully consider both the statistical significance and effect size when drawing conclusions about the meaning of their findings.

SUMMARY

Throughout this book, we have attempted to provide students, researchers and practitioners with a foundation for understanding the various methods of quantitative analysis that are currently available. Our guidance has focused on the factors that one needs to consider, the steps that one should take and the decisions that one must make when engaging in quantitative analysis. One may now appreciate that choices about quantitative analyses are never simple. They involve a consideration of one's epistemological position, the research design and the nature of the data. It is these interrelationships and conceptual aspects that form the core of choices about quantitative analysis. However, these critical aspects are often overlooked in many treatments of quantitative analysis.

With the wide availability of software that enables non-experts to conduct quantitative analyses, it is has never been more important to understand one's choices about quantitative analyses. Quantitative analyses are a powerful tool that can provide insights about a wide range of research questions. However, they are also a tool that can lead to many incorrect conclusions with substantial consequences for science, business and society (Huff, 1954). Following the criteria presented in this chapter, researchers need to use quantitative analysis with some caution and thoughtful reflection about what they can and cannot do. This is what ultimately separates those who use quantitative analysis from those who understand it. We hope that readers of this book will strive to be among the latter group.

GLOSSARY

Alpha (α)   The probability associated with a *Type I error* in null hypothesis significance testing. *Also see*: Type I error.

Alternative hypothesis   A statement about the existence of relationships or differences or associations in populations that the researcher hopes to find; also called the research hypothesis. *Also see*: Null hypothesis.

Analysis of variance (ANOVA)   A parametric analysis for examining differences between two or more means when two or more conditions or levels of the independent variable are being compared, and the dependent variable is measured using an interval or ratio measurement scale.

Archival data source   Data used by a researcher that were originally collected for some other purpose; also referred to as secondary data. *Also see*: Primary data source; Secondary data source.

Bar chart   A graphical representation of a frequency table when the data may not be continuous or are measured on a nominal, ordinal, interval scale.

Beta (β)   The probability associated with a *Type II error* in null hypothesis significance testing. *Also see*: Type II error.

Between-subjects design   A research design in which participants are included in only one of the conditions of the experiment. *Also see*: Within-subjects design.

Between-subjects variance   Variance attributable to between-group differences in the context of an ANOVA. *Also see*: Analysis of variance; Within-subjects variance.

Biserial correlation   A correlation that can be computed when both variables are ordinal. *Also see*: Correlation.

Boxplot   A graph representing the middle 50% of a distribution as a box and the upper and lower 25% as lines attached to the box.

Chi-square test of independence   A non-parametric analysis for testing the association between variables when the design of the study is between-subjects, any number of conditions of the independent variable are being compared (i.e. it can be used with just two or more than two) and the dependent variable is measured using a nominal scale.

Cluster sampling   A probability sampling method in which a higher level grouping, called a cluster, is sampled and then data is collected from the individual elements in the selected clusters. *Also see*: Probability sampling.

Constructs   Abstractions developed to explain differences, commonalities or patterns in the properties or attributes of objects, events or people.

Convenience sampling   A non-probability sampling method in which the sample is constructed using whomever may be readily available to the researcher. *Also see*: Non-probability sampling.

Correlation   An analysis for a standardized index of the direction and magnitude of the relationship between two variables on the same or different scales of measurement.

Covariance   A non-standardized index of the direction and magnitude of the relationship between two variables on the same or different scales of measurement.

Criterion   A variable that is an outcome to be predicted. A criterion in non-experimental research is analogous to a dependent variable in experimental research. *Also see*: Predictor.

Critical value   The value from a sampling distribution of a statistic that serves as the threshold for rejecting the null hypothesis. *Also see*: Null hypothesis significance testing.

Degrees of freedom   The number of values in a data set that are free to vary when computing the components of the formula for the quantitative analyses.

Dependent variable   A variable that is measured by the researcher in all types of research designs. *Also see*: Independent variable.

Descriptive quantitative analyses   Techniques that can be used to condense large amounts of data into a smaller set of numbers representing what is typical in a set of data and the amount of variability in the data.

Effect size   A standardized index of the magnitude of a difference, association or relationship.

Epistemology   The philosophical study of the nature of knowledge and how it can be created. *Also see*: Ontology.

Expected frequency   The frequency that would be expected based on the percentage in the population for a given category.

Experiment   A research design in which the researcher manipulates an independent variable and randomly assigns individuals to conditions of the experiment.

F-test   An analysis conducted to determine the difference between two or more means as part of an analysis of variance (ANOVA). Also used to test for significance of regression equations. *Also see*: Analysis of variance.

Falsification principle   The position that theories and hypotheses can never be proven true, they can only be proven false.

Frequency   The count of the number of observations at each observed value of a variable.

Histogram   A graphical representation of a frequency table when the data are continuous and on an interval or ratio scale of measurement.

Hypotheses   Testable statements about the anticipated relationships, associations or differences between variables in the population.

Independent t-test   A parametric analysis for testing the difference between two means when the research design is between-subjects, only two conditions or levels of the independent variable are being compared and the dependent variable is measured using an interval or ratio measurement scale.

Independent variable   A variable that is manipulated by the researcher in experimental and quasi-experimental research. *Also see*: Dependent variable.

Inferential quantitative analyses   Analyses designed to support inferences about a population from data obtained from a sample of that population using null hypotheses and probability.

Inter-quartile range   The middle 50% of a distribution (i.e. the 25th to 75th percentile in a distribution).

Interaction   The joint influence of two or more independent variables on a dependent variable.

Interval scale of measurement   A scale of measurement that uses numbers to capture rank order and the distance between any two units of measurement is equivalent, but the numbers do not contain a true zero point. *Also see*: Scales of measurement.

Kolmogorov-Smirnov test   An analysis that can determine if an observed distribution differs from a normal distribution, uniform distribution, exponential distribution or Poisson distribution.

Kurtosis   A statistic that reflects the degree to which a distribution is pointed or flat relative to a symmetric distribution.

Main effect   The independent influence of an independent variable on a dependent variable.

Mann-Whitney *U*   A non-parametric analysis for testing the differences in medians and ranks of the data when the design of the study is between-subjects, only two conditions or levels of the independent variable are being compared and the dependent variable is measured using an ordinal measurement scale.

Mean   The arithmetic average of a set of data.

Measurement   The assignment of numbers to properties or attributes of objects, events or people according to a set of rules.

Median   The value in the data that divides the distribution into two equal halves and represents the 50th percentile for a set of data.

Mode   The most commonly occurring value for a set of data (i.e. the most frequent value).

Multi-modal   A distribution containing more than one mode.

Multi-stage sampling   A variant of cluster analyses in which clusters are randomly sampled at the first stage and then elements within the cluster (e.g. narrower clusters or individual elements) are randomly sampled in the following stages. *Also see*: Probability sampling.

Multiple regression   An analysis for constructing equations for the best fitting line through a scatterplot using multiple predictors.

Negatively skewed distribution   A distribution following a pattern of the tail of the distribution pointing toward the lower end of the possible values for a variable. *Also see*: Positively skewed distribution.

Nominal scale of measurement   A scale of measurement that uses numbers to represent distinct categories, but the numbers have no inherent meaning. *Also see*: Scales of measurement.

Non-experiment   A research design in which there is no manipulation of the independent variable.

Non-parametric quantitative analyses   Analyses that do not assume that the underlying population takes the form of a particular distribution that has known characteristics. *Also see*: Parametric quantitative analyses.

Non-probability sampling   Sampling methods in which the probability of selecting an element into the sample is unknown.

Null hypothesis   A statement that there is no relationship or difference or association; it is the hypothesis that is directly tested in quantitative analyses. *Also see*: Alternative hypothesis; research hypothesis.

Observed frequency   The actual frequency observed in a set of data as part of a chi-square analysis.

One-tailed test   A directional hypothesis in which the direction of the difference between two variables is specified. *Also see*: Two-tailed test.

Ontology   The philosophical study of the nature of reality and how it can be studied. *Also see*: Epistemology.

Ordinal scale of measurement   A scale of measurement that uses numbers to capture rank order, but the distance between the numbers is unknown and not fixed. *Also see*: Scales of measurement.

Ordinary least squares regression   A common set of regression formulas that minimize the squared difference on average between the predicted and actual values of the criterion.

Outliers   Extreme scores in a set of data.

Paired t-test   A parametric analysis for testing the difference between two means when the research design is within-subjects, only two conditions or levels of the independent variable are being compared and the dependent variable is measured using an interval or ratio measurement scale.

Parametric quantitative analyses   Analyses that assume that the underlying population takes the form of a particular distribution that has known characteristics. *Also
see*: Non-parametric quantitative analyses.

Partial correlation   An analysis for indexing the direction and magnitude of the
relationship between two variables on the same or different scales of measurement
while statistically parcelling out the effects of a third variable. *Also see*: Correlation.

Phi coefficient   A correlation that can be computed when both variables are dichotomous (denoted φ). *Also see*: Correlation.

Point biserial correlation   A correlation that can be computed when one variable
is dichotomous and the other variable is measured on an interval or ratio scale. *Also
see*: Correlation.

Pooled variance   A sample size weighted average of the variances of two independent groups.

Population   The entire group of interest for a specific research question.

Positively skewed distribution   A distribution following a pattern of the tail of the
distribution pointing toward the higher end of the possible values for a variable. *Also
see*: Negatively skewed distribution.

Post hoc test   Parametric analysis for testing the difference between two means
when an ANOVA is statistically significant.

Predictor   A variable that is used to predict an outcome. A predictor variable in non-
experimental research is analogous to an independent variable in experimental and
quasi-experimental research. *Also see*: Criterion.

Primary data source   Data collected by a researcher as part of a specific research
study. *Also see*: Archival data source; Secondary data source.

Probability   The likelihood of a particular outcome occurring with a range of 0.00
(no chance of an outcome occurring) to 1.00 (the outcome is certain to occur).

Probability sampling   Sampling methods in which each element of the sample frame
has a non-zero probability of being selected into the sample and the probability is known.

Purposeful sampling   A non-probability sampling method in which an expert identifies specific elements or clusters that will be representative of the population. *Also
see*: Non-probability sampling.

Quantitative analysis　Procedures and rules used to reduce large amounts of data into more manageable forms that allow one to draw conclusions and insights about patterns in the data.

Quasi-experiment　A research design which includes a manipulation of an independent variable, but the assignment of individuals to conditions of the experiment is not random or the manipulation is not controlled by the researcher.

Quota sampling　A non-probability sampling method in which a fixed number of sample elements with particular characteristics are sampled. *Also see*: Non-probability sampling.

Random assignment　Using a random process to determine which individuals are assigned to the different conditions in an experiment.

Range　The total variability on a variable demarcated by the distance from the largest and smallest value in a set of data.

Rank biserial correlation　A correlation that can be computed when one variable is a rank (ordinal) and the other variable is on an interval or ratio scale of measurement. *Also see*: Correlation.

Ratio scale of measurement　A scale of measurement that uses numbers to capture rank order, the distance between any two units of measurement is equivalent and the numbers contain a true zero point. *Also see*: Scales of measurement.

Research hypothesis　A statement about the existence of relationships or differences or associations in populations that the researcher hopes to find; also called the alternative hypothesis. *Also see*: Null hypothesis.

Sample　A subset of the populations selected to participate in the research. *Also see*: Population.

Sample size　The number of observations in a data set to be used in a given quantitative analysis.

Sampling　The process by which the sample is identified and selected.

Sampling distribution　A distribution of a statistic that is used to compute the probabilities used in null hypothesis significance testing.

Sampling error　The degree to which the sample statistics differ to the corresponding parameters in the population.

Sampling frame   A list of individual elements in a population that can be used to sample the elements.

Scales of measurement   The nature of the numeric qualities of the numbers that are assigned to the properties or attributes of objects, events or people.

Scatterplot   A graph simultaneously plotting the location of two variables on a two-dimensional plane.

Secondary data source   Data used by a researcher that were originally collected for some other purpose; also referred to as archival data. *Also see*: Archival data source; Primary data source.

Shapiro-Wilks test   An analysis that can determine if an observed distribution differs from a normal distribution and is particularly useful when sample sizes are small.

Simple random sampling   A probability sampling method in which each element of the sampling frame has an equal probability of being selected into the sample. *Also see*: Probability sampling.

Simple regression   An analysis for constructing equations for the best fitting line through a scatterplot using a single predictor.

Single-factor independent ANOVA   A parametric analysis for testing the difference between means when the research design is between-subjects, there are more than two conditions or levels of the independent variable being compared, there is only one independent variable and the dependent variable is measured using an interval or ratio measurement scale.

Single-factor repeated-measures ANOVA   A parametric analysis for testing the difference between means when the research design is within-subjects, there are more than two conditions or levels of the independent variable being compared, there is only one independent variable and the dependent variable is measured using an interval or ratio measurement scale.

Skewness   A statistic that reflects the degree to which a distribution is symmetric.

Snowball sampling   A non-probability sampling technique in which an initial sample is contacted to participate and then asked to send an invitation to participate in the study to others in their social and professional networks. *Also see*: Non-probability sampling.

Spearman's Rho   A correlation that can be computed when both variables are measured as ranks. *Also see*: Correlation.

Standard deviation   The average deviation of the datum points from the mean and the square root of the variance.

Standard error of the mean   The standard deviation of a sampling distribution of means.

Statistical power   The probability of correctly rejecting the null hypothesis when it is false in the population (1-β). *Also see*: Beta.

Steam and leaf plot   A graphical representation of a frequency table in which the graph is presented vertically and is constructed using the actual values in the data by using the leading digit of a number as the stem in the graph and the trailing digit to create the leaves.

Stratified sampling   A probability sampling method in which the sampling frame is divided into strata based on characteristics of the elements and then random sampling is conducted in each strata. *Also see*: Probability sampling.

Symmetrical distribution   A distribution following a symmetrical pattern in which the right and left sides of the distribution are mirror images of one another.

Systematic sampling   A probability sampling method in which the selection of elements from the sampling frame is not completely at random and a repeating pattern of a fixed interval is used to select the sample from the sampling frame. *Also see*: Probability sampling.

Two-factor independent ANOVA   A parametric analysis for testing the difference between means when the research design is between-subjects, there are more than two conditions or levels of the independent variable being compared, there is more than one independent variable and the dependent variable is measured using an interval or ratio measurement scale.

Two-tailed test   A non-directional hypothesis in which the direction of the difference, association or relationship is not specified. *Also see*: One-tailed test.

Type I error   An incorrect decision about the null hypothesis in which one rejects the null hypothesis when it is true in the population and it should not be rejected. *Also see*: Alpha.

Type II error   An incorrect decision about the null hypothesis in which one fails to reject the null hypothesis when it is false in the population and it should be rejected. *Also see*: Beta.

Variables   Properties or attributes of objects, events or people that can take on different values.

Variance   The average squared deviation of the datum points from the mean.

Within-subjects design   A research design in which participants are included in more than one of the conditions of the experiment (also called repeated-measures designs). *Also see*: Between-subjects design.

Within-subjects variance   Variance attributable to differences between individuals within groups in the context of an ANOVA. *Also see*: Analysis of variance; Between-subjects variance.

Z-score   A standardized score which represents the number of standard deviations a datum point is from the mean.

APPENDIX: EXCEL FORMULAS

Quantitative Analysis	Excel Function	Description
Chi-square	=CHISQ.TEST(actual range, expected range)	This function computes the chi-square. To use this function, one must identify the observed frequencies and the expected frequencies.
Chi-square distribution	=CHISQ.DIST.RT(chi-square value, df)	This function computes the probability associated with a chi-square test on a set of data. To use this function, one must specify the value of the chi-square and the degrees of freedom.
Correlation	=CORREL(variable 1 data, variable 2 data)	This function computes the Pearson correlation.
Cumulative frequency	=FREQUENCY(variable data, value to count)	This function computes the cumulative frequency for a specific value of a variable.
F-distribution	=F.DIST.RT(F value, df between, df within)	This function computes the probability associated with an F-test on a set of data. To use this function, one must specify the value of the F-statistic, the degrees of freedom between, and the degrees of freedom within.
Frequency	=COUNTIF(variable data, value to count)	This function computes the frequency for a specific value of a variable.
Kurtosis	=KURT(variable data)	This function computes the kurtosis of a set of data.
Maximum	=MAX(variable data)	This function computes the maximum value in a set of data.
Mean	=AVERAGE(variable data)	This function computes the mean of a set of data.
Median	=MEDIAN(variable data)	This function computes the median of a set of data.
Minimum	=MIN(variable data)	This function computes the minimum value in a set of data.
Mode	=MODE(variable data)	This function computes the mode of a set of data.
Regression	=linest(Y variable data, X variable data, include constant, report statistics)	This function computes the simple or multiple ordinary least squares regression equation including all associated statistical tests. To use this function, one must identify the data for the Y variable and the data for the X variable.

(Continued)

(Continued)

Quantitative Analysis	Excel Function	Description
		One indicates if an intercept should (TRUE) or should not (FALSE) be included in the model. Also, one indicates whether the associated statistics should (TRUE) or should not (FALSE) be computed. The statistics reported include the standard error for each regression term, R-squared, and the standard error of the estimate. To run this function, one must press CTRL+SHIFT+ENTER when the formula components have been entered.
R-squared	=RSQ(Y variable data, X variable data)	This function computes the squared correlation coefficient.
Skewness	=SKEW(variable data)	This function computes the skewness of a set of data.
Standard deviation	=STDEV.S(variable data)	This function computes the standard deviation of a set of data using the calculation for a sample.
t-distribution	=T.DIST.2T (calculated t-value, df)	This function computes the probability associated with a t-test on a set of data. To use this function, one must specify the value of the t-statistic and the degrees of freedom.
t-test	=T.TEST(data for group 1, data for group 2, tails, type of t-test)	This function computes the probability associated with a t-test on a set of data. It computes the probability directly and does not report the t-value. To use this function, one must specify whether it is a one- or two-tailed hypothesis for the tails option by entering 1 or 2. One must also indicate the type of t-test. The options include a paired t-test (1), an independent t-test where the homogeneity of variance is met (2), and an independent t-test where the homogeneity of variance is not met (3).
Variance	=VAR.S(variable data)	This function computes the variance of a set of data using the calculation for a sample.
z-distribution	=NORM.S.DIST(Z,True)	This function computes the probability associated with a z-score. To use this function, one must specify the value of the z-statistic and the type of probability computation with TRUE returning the cumulative probability function and FALSE returning the probability density function.
z-score	=STANDARDIZE(score, mean, standard deviation)	This function computes the z-score for a given mean and standard deviation. To use this function, one must identify the score, the mean and the standard deviation.

REFERENCES

Abelson, R. P. (1985) 'A variance explanation paradox: When a little is a lot', *Psychological Bulletin*, 97(1): 129-33.

Abelson, R. P. (1995) *Statistics as Principled Argument*. Hillsdale, NJ: Lawrence Erlbaum.

Abelson, R. P. (1997) 'On the surprising longevity of flogged horses: Why there is a case for the significance test', *Psychological Science*, 8(1): 12-15.

Aguinis, H. and Edwards, J. R. (2014) 'Methodological wishes for the next decade and how to make wishes come true', *Journal of Management Studies*, 51(1): 143-74.

Aguinis, H. and Vandenberg, R. J. (2014) 'An ounce of prevention is worth a pound of cure: Improving research quality before data collection', *Annual Review of Organizational Psychology and Organizational Behavior*, 1: 569-95.

Aguinis, H., Werner, S., Abbott, J. L., Angert, C., Park, J. H., and Kohlhausen, D. (2010) 'Customer-centric science: Reporting significant research results with rigor, relevance, and practical impact in mind', *Organizational Research Methods*, 13(3): 515-39.

Alison, P. (2001) *Missing Data*. Thousand Oaks, CA: Sage.

Austin, J., Boyle, K., and Lualhati, J. (1998) 'Statistical conclusion validity for organizational science researchers: A review', *Organizational Research Methods*, 1(2): 164-208.

Ayers, I. (2008) *Super Crunchers: Why Thinking-By-Numbers is the New Way To Be Smart*. New York: Bantam.

Baughn, C., Neupert, K., and Sugheir, J. (2013) 'Domestic migration and new business creation in the United States', *Journal of Small Business & Entrepreneurship*, 26(1): 1-14.

Buchanan, D. and Bryman, A. (2007) 'Contextualizing methods choice in organizational research', *Organizational Research Methods*, 10(3): 483-501.

Buchanan, D. and Bryman, A. (2009) 'The organizational research context: Properties and implications', in D. Buchanan and A. Bryman (eds), *Handbook of Organizational Research Methods*. London: Sage, pp. 636-53.

Campion, M. A. (1993) 'Article review checklist: A criterion checklist for reviewing research articles in applied psychology', *Personnel Psychology*, 46: 705-18.

Carver, R. P. (1993) 'The case against statistical significance testing, revisited', *Journal of Experimental Education*, 61(4): 287-92.

Cashen, L. and Geiger, S. (2004) 'Statistical power and the testing of null hypotheses: A review of contemporary management research and recommendations for future studies', *Organizational Research Methods*, 7(2): 151-67.

Cohen, J. (1988) *Statistical Power Analysis for the Behavioral Sciences*. Hillsdale, NJ: Lawrence Erlbaum.

Cohen, J. (1992) 'A power primer', *Psychological Bulletin*, 112(1): 155-9.

Cohen, J. (1994) 'The earth is round (p <.05)', *American Psychologist*, 49(12): 997-1003.

Cohen, J., Cohen, P., West, S. G., and Aiken, L. S. (2003) *Applied Multiple Regression/ Correlation Analysis for the Behavioral Sciences* (3rd edn). Hillsdale, NJ: Lawrence Erlbaum.

Combs, J. G. (2010) 'Big samples and small effects: Let's not trade relevance and rigor for power', *Academy of Management Journal*, 53(1): 9-13.

Cook, T. D. and Campbell, D. T. (1979) *Quasi-Experimentation: Design and Analysis Issues for Field Settings*. Boston: Houghton Mifflin.

Cortina, J. and Landis, R. (2011) 'The earth is not round (p = .00)', *Organizational Research Methods*, 14(2): 332-49.

Davenport, T. and Harris, J. (2007) *Competing on Analytics: The New Science of Winning*. Boston: Harvard Business Press.

Davenport, T. and Patil, D. (2012) 'Data scientist: The sexiest job of the 21st century', *Harvard Business Review*, 90(10): 70-6.

DeCarlo, L. T. (1997) 'On the meaning and use of kurtosis', *Psychological Methods*, 2(2): 292-307.

Deetz, S. (1996) 'Describing differences in approaches to organization science: Rethinking Burrell and Morgan and their legacy', *Organizational Science*, 7(2): 191-207.

Desrosiers, E., Sherony, K., Barros, E., Ballinger, G., Senol, S., and Campion, M. (2002) 'Writing research articles: Update to the article review checklist', in S. G. Rogelberg (ed.), *Handbook of Research Methods in Industrial and Organizational Psychology*. London: Blackwell, pp. 459-78.

Economist, The (2010) 'The data deluge', 25 February.

Edwards, J. R. (2008) 'To prosper, organizational psychology should ... overcome methodological barriers to progress', *Journal of Organizational Behaviour*, 29(4): 469-91.

Edwards, J. R. and Berry, J. W. (2010) 'The presence of something or the absence of nothing: Increasing theoretical precision in management research', *Organizational Research Methods*, 13(4): 668-89.

Faul, F., Erdfelder, E., Lang, A.G., and Buchner, A. (2007) 'G*Power 3: A flexible statistical power analysis for the social, behavioral, and biomedical sciences', *Behavior
Research Methods*, 39(2): 175–91.

Field, A. (2013) *Discovering Statistics using IBM SPSS Statistics*. London: Sage.

Fisher, R. A. (1938) 'Presidential address by Professor R. A. Fisher, Sc.D., F.R.S.', *The
Indian Journal of Statistics*, 4(1): 14–17.

Frick, R. W. (1996) 'The appropriate use of null hypothesis testing', *Psychological
Methods*, 1(2): 379–90.

Gibbons, J. D. (1993) *Nonparametric Statistics: An Introduction*. Thousand Oaks, CA:
Sage.

Graham, J. (2009) 'Missing data analysis: Making it work in the real world', *Annual
Review of Psychology*, 60: 549–76.

Grant, A. (2012) 'Leading with meaning: Beneficiary contact, prosocial impact, and
the performance effects of transformational leadership', *Academy of Management
Journal*, 55(2): 458–76.

Greenberg, J. (1987) 'The college sophomore as guinea pig: Setting the record
straight', *Academy of Management Review*, 12(1): 157–9.

Griskevicius, V., Tybur, J., and Van den Bergh, B. (2010) 'Going green to be seen:
Status, reputation, and conspicuous consumption', *Journal of Personality and
Social Psychology*, 98: 392–404.

Harlow, L., Muliak, S., and Steiger, J. (eds) (1997) *What If There Were No Significance
Tests?* Mahwah, NJ: Lawrence Erlbaum.

Hox, J. J. and Boeije, H. R. (2005) 'Data collection, primary versus secondary', in
K. Kempf-Leonard (ed.). *Encyclopedia of Social Measurement*. San Diego, CA:
Academic Press, pp. 593–9.

Huff, D. (1954) *How to Lie with Statistics*. New York: W. W. Norton.

Kalton, G. (1983) *Introduction to Survey Sampling*. Thousand Oaks, CA: Sage.

Kline, R. (2004) *Beyond Significance Testing: Reforming Data Analysis Methods in
Behavioral Research*. Washington, DC: American Psychological Association.

Lance, C. E., Butts, M. M., and Michels, L. C. (2006) 'The sources of four commonly
reported cutoff criteria: What did they really say?', *Organizational Research
Methods*, 9(2): 202–20.

Lee, L., Wong, P., Foo, M., and Leung A. (2011) 'Entrepreneurial intentions: The influence of organizational and individual factors', *Journal of Business Venturing*, 26(1):
124–36.

Lehman, E. (2011) *Fisher, Neyman, and the Creation of Classical Statistics*. New York:
Springer.

Lewis, M. (2004) *Moneyball: The Art of Winning an Unfair Game*. New York: W. W.
Norton.

Little, R. and Rubin, D. (2002) *Statistical Analysis with Missing Data* (2nd edn). New
York: Wiley.

McAfee, A. and Brynjolfsson, E. (2012) 'Big data: The management revolution', *Harvard Business Review*, 90(10): 60–8.

Mayer-Schönberger, V. and Cukier, K. (2013) *Big Data: A Revolution that Will Transform How We Live, Work, and Think*. Boston: Houghton Mifflin Harcourt.

Meehl, P. E. (1978) 'Theoretical risks and tabular asterisks: Sir Karl, Sir Ronald, and the slow progress of soft psychology', *Journal of Consulting and Clinical Psychology*, 46(4): 806–34.

Meehl, P. (1990) 'Appraising and amending theories: The strategy of Lakatosian defense and two principles that warrant it', *Psychological Inquiry*, 1(2): 108–41.

Menard, S. (2008) *Handbook of Longitudinal Research: Design, Measurement, and Analysis*. San Diego, CA: Academic Press.

Murphy, K. and Myors, B. (1998) *Statistical Power Analysis: A Simple and General Model for Traditional and Modern Hypothesis Tests*. Mahwah, NJ: Lawrence Erlbaum.

Murray, H. A. (1938) *Explorations in Personality*. New York: Oxford University Press.

Nunnally, J. C. (1978) *Psychometric Theory* (2nd edn). New York: McGraw-Hill.

Parker, R. A. and Berman, N. G. (2003) 'Sample size: More than calculations', *American Statistician*, 57: 166.

Pedhazur, E. and Pedhazur-Schmelkin, L. (1991) *Measurement, Design, and Analysis: An Integrated Approach*. New York: Psychology Press.

Pfeffer, J. and Sutton, R. (2006) 'Evidence-based management', *Harvard Business Review*, 84: 62–74.

Popper, K. (1959) *The Logic of Scientific Discovery*. New York: Routledge.

Prentice, D. A. and Miller, D. T. (1992) 'When small effects are impressive', *Psychological Bulletin*, 112(1): 160–4.

Qayyum, A. and Sukirno, M. (2012) 'An empirical analysis of employee motivation and the role of demographics: The banking industry of Pakistan', *Global Business and Management Research: An International Journal*, 4(1): 1–14.

Rosenthal, R. (1991) *Meta-Analytic Procedures for Social Research*. Newbury Park, CA: Sage.

Salsburg, D. (2002) *The Lady Tasting Tea: How Statistics Revolutionized Science in the Twentieth Century*. New York: Henry Holt & Co.

Saunders, M. N. K. (2012) 'Choosing research participants', in G. Symon and C. Cassell (eds), *Qualitative Organizational Research*. London: Sage, pp. 35–52.

Scherbaum, C. A. (2005) 'A basic guide to statistical discovery: Planning and selecting statistical analyses', in F. Leong and J. Austin (eds), *The Psychology Research Handbook: A Guide for Graduate Students and Research Assistants* (2nd edn). Thousand Oaks, CA: Sage, pp. 275–92.

Scherbaum, C. A. and Meade, A. W. (2009) 'Measurement in the organizational sciences', in D. Buchanan and A. Bryman (eds), *Handbook of Organizational Research Methods*. London: Sage, pp. 636–53.

Scherbaum, C. and Meade, A. (2013) 'New directions for measurement in management research', *International Journal of Management Reviews*, 15: 132–48.

Schmidt, F. L. and Hunter, J. E. (1997) 'Eight common but false objections to the discontinuation of significance testing in the analysis of research data', in L. Harlow, S. Muliak and J. Steiger (eds), *What if There Were No Significance Tests?* Mahwah, NJ: Lawrence Erlbaum, pp. 37–64.

Sengupta, S. and Gupta, A. (2012) 'Exploring the dimensions of attrition in Indian BPOs', *The International Journal of Human Resource Management*, 23(6): 1259–88.

Shockley, K. M. and Allen, T. D. (2010) 'Uncovering the missing link in flexible work arrangement utilization: An individual difference perspective', *Journal of Vocational Behavior*, 76: 131–42.

Shrout, P. E. (1997) 'Should significance tests be banned? Introduction to a special section exploring the pros and cons', *Psychological Science*, 8(1): 1–2.

Siegel, E. (2013) *Predictive Analytics*. New York: Wiley.

Siegel, S. and Castellan, N. (1998) *Nonparametric Statistics for the Behavioral Sciences* (2nd edn). New York: McGraw-Hill.

Stevens, S. S. (1968) 'Measurement, statistics, and schemapiric view', *Science*, 56: 849–56.

Taleb, N. (2007) *The Black Swan: The Impact of the Highly Improbable*. New York: Random House.

Tukey, J. (1977) *Exploratory Data Analysis*. Reading, MA: Addison-Wesley.

Tzelgov, J. and Henik, A. (1991) 'Suppression situations in psychological research: Definitions, implications, and applications', *Psychological Bulletin*, 109(3): 524–36.

Wagner, D. T., Barnes, C. M., Lim, V. G., and Ferris, D. (2012) 'Lost sleep and cyberloafing: Evidence from the laboratory and a daylight saving time quasi-experiment', *Journal of Applied Psychology*, 97(5): 1068–76.

Walla, P., Brenner, G., and Koller, M. (2011) 'Objective measures of emotion related to brand attitude: A new way to quantify emotion-related aspects relevant to marketing', *PLoS ONE*, 6(11): e26782. doi:10.1371/journal.pone.0026782.

Winer, J., Brown, D., and Michels, K. (1991) *Statistical Principles in Experimental Design*. New York: McGraw-Hill.

Ziliak, S. and McCloskey, D. (2008) *The Cult of Statistical Significance: How the Standard Error Costs Us Jobs, Justice, and Lives*. Ann Arbor, MI: University of Michigan Press.

INDEX

NOTE: page numbers in *italic type* refer to figures and tables, page numbers in **bold type** refer to glossary definitions.

Fold a Shark

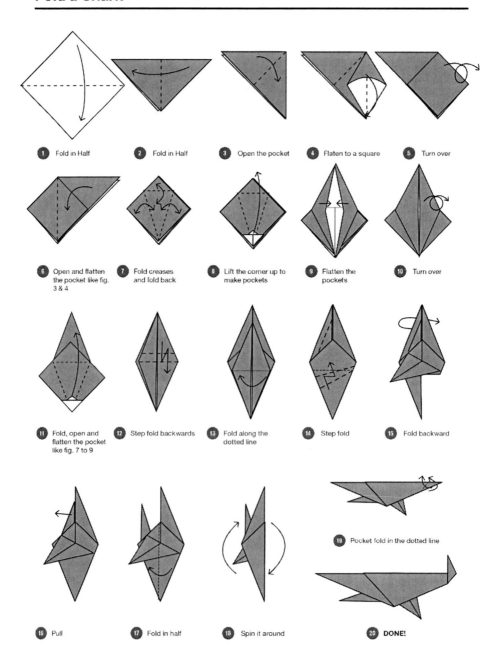

1. Fold in Half
2. Fold in Half
3. Open the pocket
4. Flaten to a square
5. Turn over
6. Open and flatten the pocket like fig. 3 & 4
7. Fold creases and fold back
8. Lift the corner up to make pockets
9. Flatten the pockets
10. Turn over
11. Fold, open and flatten the pocket like fig. 7 to 9
12. Step fold backwards
13. Fold along the dotted line
14. Step fold
15. Fold backward
16. Pull
17. Fold in half
18. Spin it around
19. Pocket fold in the dotted line
20. DONE!

CPSIA information can be obtained
at www.ICGtesting.com
Printed in the USA
LVOW09s1407100217
523870LV00011BA/247/P